The New Workplace: Mastering Remote and Hybrid Work Models

THE NEW WORKPLACE: MASTERING REMOTE AND HYBRID WORK MODELS PART 1: INTRODUCTION TO REMOTE AND HYBRID WORK 1

PART 1: INTRODUCTION TO REMOTE AND HYBRID WORK 6

1. THE EVOLUTION OF WORK MODELS 7
- HISTORICAL CONTEXT OF REMOTE AND HYBRID WORK 8
- KEY DRIVERS: TECHNOLOGY, GLOBALIZATION, AND THE PANDEMIC 9
- BENEFITS AND CHALLENGES OF DISTRIBUTED WORK 11

2. DEFINING REMOTE AND HYBRID WORK MODELS 13
- WHAT IS REMOTE WORK? 14
- WHAT IS A HYBRID WORK MODEL? 15
- COMMON VARIATIONS AND EXAMPLES IN DIFFERENT INDUSTRIES 17

3. THE FUTURE OF WORK 21
- EMERGING TRENDS IN DISTRIBUTED WORK MODELS 22
- PREDICTIONS FOR WORKPLACE DYNAMICS 27

PART 2: MANAGING DISTRIBUTED TEAMS 31

4. BUILDING AN EFFECTIVE DISTRIBUTED TEAM 32
- HIRING FOR REMOTE AND HYBRID ROLES 33
- IMPORTANCE OF DIVERSITY AND INCLUSION IN DISTRIBUTED TEAMS 38

5. LEADERSHIP STRATEGIES FOR DISTRIBUTED TEAMS 45
- ADAPTING LEADERSHIP STYLES FOR REMOTE MANAGEMENT 46
- CREATING ACCOUNTABILITY AND TRUST 50

6. COMMUNICATION AND ENGAGEMENT 54
- MANAGING COMMUNICATION ACROSS TIME ZONES 55
- BEST PRACTICES FOR VIRTUAL MEETINGS AND CHECK-INS 58
- STRATEGIES FOR BOOSTING EMPLOYEE ENGAGEMENT 60

7. PERFORMANCE MANAGEMENT IN REMOTE SETTINGS 62
- SETTING CLEAR EXPECTATIONS AND GOALS 63
- MEASURING AND EVALUATING TEAM PERFORMANCE 66

PART 3: TECHNOLOGY AND COLLABORATION TOOLS 71

8. CHOOSING THE RIGHT TOOLS 72

Overview of Popular Collaboration and Communication Platforms 73
Integration of Tools for Seamless Workflows 76

9. ENSURING SECURE AND EFFICIENT COMMUNICATION 80

Cybersecurity Considerations for Distributed Work 81
Data Protection and Privacy 84

10. LEVERAGING ADVANCED TECHNOLOGIES 88

Role of AI and Automation in Remote Work 89
Virtual and Augmented Reality for Collaboration 91

PART 4: WORK-LIFE BALANCE IN REMOTE WORK 95

11. CHALLENGES OF WORK-LIFE BALANCE IN DISTRIBUTED WORK 96

Common Struggles: Overwork, Isolation, and Burnout 97
Differences in Cultural Perceptions of Work-Life Boundaries 101

12. PROMOTING EMPLOYEE WELL-BEING 104

Mental Health Resources and Initiatives 105
Encouraging Breaks and Maintaining Work Boundaries 107

13. CREATING FLEXIBLE POLICIES FOR WORK-LIFE BALANCE 110

Crafting Policies That Support Both Employees and Organizations 111
Role of HR in Ensuring Well-Being 113

PART 5: CASE STUDIES AND BEST PRACTICES 116

14. SUCCESS STORIES IN REMOTE AND HYBRID WORK 117

Examples from Leading Companies 118
Lessons Learned: 118

15. OVERCOMING COMMON CHALLENGES 123

Strategies to Address Team Disconnect, Tech Failures, and Resistance to Change 124

16. CUSTOMIZING MODELS FOR YOUR ORGANIZATION 131

Tailoring Work Models Based on Company Size 132

PART 6: THE ROAD AHEAD 141

17. CONTINUOUS IMPROVEMENT IN REMOTE AND HYBRID WORK 142
Feedback Mechanisms and Iteration 143
Staying Agile in the Face of Changing Work Dynamics 148

18. PREPARING FOR THE FUTURE 151
Future Skills for Remote Workers and Leaders 152
Building a Resilient Organization for Distributed Work 157

19. CONCLUSION: EMBRACING CHANGE IN THE WORKPLACE 161
Recap of Key Insights 162
Call to Action for Leaders and Employees 165

Remote and Hybrid Work Model

Part 1: Introduction to Remote and Hybrid Work

1. The Evolution of Work Models

Historical Context of Remote and Hybrid Work

The concept of remote work is not a new phenomenon, although its widespread adoption is relatively recent. Historically, most work was conducted within local communities, often at home or within close-knit workshops. In the pre-industrial era, agrarian economies relied heavily on family-based production systems, where work and life were inseparable. The Industrial Revolution in the 18th and 19th centuries, however, marked a seismic shift in how work was organized. Factories became the dominant workplace, demanding centralized labor forces and rigid schedules.

The rise of office jobs in the early 20th century further entrenched the notion of centralized workplaces. Employees commuted to offices to collaborate, access resources, and maintain productivity. This model persisted for decades, underpinned by technological constraints that required physical presence for communication and production.

The seeds of remote work as we know it were planted in the mid-20th century with advances in telecommunications. The invention of the telephone, fax machine, and later, personal computers laid the groundwork for decentralized work. By the late 20th century, the concept of "telecommuting" emerged, championed as a solution to urban congestion and environmental concerns. Organizations began experimenting with flexible work arrangements, but these were often limited to a small segment of the workforce.

The 21st century ushered in a technological revolution that fundamentally reshaped the workplace. High-speed internet, cloud computing, and mobile devices allowed employees to work from virtually anywhere. Remote work became increasingly viable, though still viewed as a perk rather than a standard practice. The COVID-19 pandemic in 2020 acted as a catalyst, forcing organizations worldwide to embrace remote and hybrid work models almost overnight. What began as a temporary measure has since evolved into a lasting transformation, reshaping societal and corporate perceptions of work.

Key Drivers: Technology, Globalization, and the Pandemic

Technology

Advances in technology have been the most significant enabler of remote and hybrid work. High-speed internet and mobile technology provide the foundation for distributed teams. Collaboration tools such as Zoom, Microsoft Teams, and Slack have become integral to workplace communication, while project management platforms like Trello, Asana, and Jira ensure alignment and accountability.

Artificial Intelligence (AI) and automation have further streamlined processes, allowing teams to work asynchronously. For example, automated scheduling tools and AI-driven analytics enable efficient operations regardless of time zones. Virtual reality (VR) and augmented reality (AR) technologies are emerging as the next frontier, offering immersive solutions for remote training, meetings, and team-building exercises.

Globalization

Globalization has expanded the reach of businesses, enabling them to tap into talent pools worldwide. Distributed workforces became a necessity for multinational corporations seeking to operate across different regions and time zones. This trend has also benefited employees, who now have access to opportunities far beyond their geographic location.

Outsourcing and offshoring, facilitated by global connectivity, are prime examples of how work transcends borders. Remote work models have democratized access to talent, allowing companies to diversify their teams and foster innovation through varied perspectives.

The COVID-19 Pandemic

The pandemic was an inflection point for remote work adoption. As governments imposed lockdowns to curb the spread of COVID-19, businesses had no choice but to pivot to remote operations. This sudden shift revealed both the potential and the challenges of distributed work.

Organizations quickly realized that many roles could be performed remotely without compromising productivity. Employees, on the other hand, appreciated the flexibility and reduced commuting time. However, the abrupt transition also highlighted issues such as digital fatigue, inadequate infrastructure, and the need for robust cybersecurity measures.

Post-pandemic, many companies have adopted hybrid work models, blending in-office and remote work to balance flexibility with collaboration. This period has underscored the importance of adaptability and innovation in the evolving workplace landscape.

Benefits and Challenges of Distributed Work

Benefits

Flexibility: Remote and hybrid work models offer employees greater control over their schedules, allowing for improved work-life balance.

Cost Savings: Businesses can reduce overhead costs associated with maintaining office spaces, while employees save on commuting and related expenses.

Access to Talent: Companies can recruit from a global talent pool, enhancing diversity and expertise within their teams.

Increased Productivity: Many employees report being more productive when working remotely due to fewer workplace distractions and the ability to tailor their environments.

Environmental Impact: Reduced commuting contributes to lower greenhouse gas emissions, aligning with sustainability goals.

Challenges

Communication Barriers: Misunderstandings and delays can arise when teams operate across time zones and rely heavily on digital communication.

Employee Isolation: Lack of social interaction can lead to feelings of loneliness and disengagement.

Management Difficulties: Supervising distributed teams requires new skills and tools to ensure accountability and cohesion.

Cybersecurity Risks: Remote work increases vulnerability to cyberattacks, necessitating robust security measures.

Work-Life Balance Issues: While flexibility is a benefit, it can also blur boundaries between personal and professional life, leading to burnout.

In conclusion, the evolution of work models reflects a dynamic interplay of technological, economic, and societal forces. As remote and hybrid work continue to gain traction, understanding their historical context and key drivers is essential for navigating the challenges and opportunities they present. By leveraging technology and fostering adaptability, organizations and employees can thrive in this new era of work.

2. Defining Remote and Hybrid Work Models

What is Remote Work?

Remote work, also known as telecommuting or work-from-home, refers to a professional arrangement where employees perform their job responsibilities outside of traditional office spaces. This setup enables individuals to work from a variety of locations, such as their homes, coworking spaces, coffee shops, or even while traveling. Remote work is characterized by its reliance on technology to facilitate communication, collaboration, and task completion without the need for physical presence in a centralized office.

The concept of remote work is grounded in flexibility. Employees are often allowed to set their own schedules within the boundaries of agreed-upon deadlines and expectations. This flexibility extends beyond work hours to include choices about the work environment, which can be tailored to individual preferences. The underlying goal of remote work is to prioritize outcomes and productivity over physical presence.

Remote work typically requires robust technological infrastructure. High-speed internet is the foundation, allowing seamless access to digital tools and platforms. Collaboration software such as Slack, Microsoft Teams, and Zoom enables teams to stay connected, while cloud-based systems provide access to essential files and applications. Cybersecurity measures, such as virtual private networks (VPNs) and two-factor authentication, are critical to protecting sensitive company data.

The benefits of remote work are manifold. Employees save time and money by eliminating commutes, which can also contribute to improved mental well-being. Organizations can reduce overhead costs associated with maintaining office spaces, including utilities and real estate expenses. Additionally, remote work supports inclusivity by accommodating individuals with disabilities or caregiving responsibilities.

However, remote work is not without challenges. Employees may experience feelings of isolation or disconnection from their teams. Communication can be hindered by time zone differences, and some individuals may struggle with self-discipline in a less structured environment. For organizations, managing a remote workforce requires a shift in leadership strategies, with an emphasis on trust, transparency, and measurable performance outcomes.

In conclusion, remote work is a transformative model that leverages technology to decouple productivity from physical location. Its adoption continues to grow as both employees and organizations recognize its potential to enhance flexibility, efficiency, and inclusivity in the modern workplace.

What is a Hybrid Work Model?

The hybrid work model is a flexible arrangement that combines elements of both remote and in-office work. In this setup, employees split their time between working from a designated office location and a remote environment. The balance between these modes varies depending on organizational policies, job roles, and individual preferences. Hybrid work aims to blend the benefits of remote work—such as flexibility and reduced commuting—with the advantages of in-person collaboration and team building.

Hybrid work models gained prominence following the COVID-19 pandemic, as organizations sought to strike a balance between operational continuity and employee well-being. While some companies established formal hybrid policies, others adopted a more fluid approach, allowing teams or individuals to determine their schedules.

One key feature of the hybrid model is its adaptability. Organizations can customize their approach based on business needs, team dynamics, and employee expectations. For example, some companies implement fixed schedules where employees are required to work in the office on specific days, while others operate on a "flexible hybrid" basis, granting employees autonomy over their location.

Hybrid work models address many of the challenges associated with fully remote or fully in-office work. For example, employees can enjoy the flexibility of remote work while still benefiting from in-person mentorship, brainstorming sessions, and social interactions. This balance can boost morale, foster innovation, and strengthen team cohesion.

However, implementing a hybrid model is not without its complexities. Organizations must invest in technology to support seamless transitions between remote and in-office work. This includes equipping office spaces with video conferencing capabilities and ensuring that remote employees have access to the same resources as their in-office counterparts. Clear communication and defined expectations are also crucial to avoiding misunderstandings and ensuring equity among team members.

Hybrid work models also require a cultural shift. Leaders must focus on outcomes rather than hours worked or physical presence, and they must work to create an inclusive environment where remote employees feel as engaged and valued as those in the office.

In summary, the hybrid work model offers a middle ground that combines the flexibility of remote work with the benefits of in-person interaction. By embracing this approach, organizations can create a dynamic and resilient workforce that is well-equipped to navigate the challenges of a rapidly changing world.

Common Variations and Examples in Different Industries

Remote and hybrid work models are not one-size-fits-all; their implementation varies widely across industries based on the nature of work, organizational culture, and technological infrastructure. These variations reflect the diverse ways in which industries have adapted to the evolving demands of the modern workplace.

In the technology sector, remote and hybrid work models have become the norm. Tech companies often prioritize flexibility to attract top talent, many of whom value the ability to work from anywhere. Examples include companies like GitLab and Automattic, which operate fully remote models, and Microsoft and Google, which have adopted hybrid policies. In these organizations, collaboration tools, cloud platforms, and advanced cybersecurity measures play a pivotal role in enabling distributed workforces.

The creative industries, such as marketing, advertising, and design, also benefit from flexible work arrangements. Creative professionals often collaborate on projects that require brainstorming and ideation, which can be conducted both in person and virtually. Agencies may host periodic in-person workshops while allowing day-to-day tasks to be completed remotely. Hybrid models are particularly effective in fostering creativity while accommodating diverse work styles.

In the finance and banking sector, hybrid models are gaining traction, though with more structured approaches. Tasks such as data analysis and reporting can be completed remotely, while activities requiring face-to-face interaction, such as client meetings, are conducted in the office. For example, JPMorgan Chase has implemented a hybrid model that combines remote work for back-office roles with in-office work for client-facing employees.

The healthcare industry presents a unique case. While clinical roles require physical presence, administrative and support functions can often be performed remotely. Telemedicine has expanded significantly, enabling healthcare professionals to consult with patients virtually. Hybrid models are also used in medical research and education, where remote collaboration is complemented by in-person laboratory work and clinical training.

The education sector has embraced hybrid models in response to shifting demands. Remote learning platforms allow educators to deliver lectures and interact with students virtually, while in-person sessions are reserved for activities such as laboratory experiments, group discussions, and exams. Universities and schools have adopted blended learning approaches to cater to diverse student needs.

The manufacturing and logistics industry relies heavily on physical presence for production and operations. However, hybrid models are being introduced for roles such as supply chain management, planning, and administrative tasks. Employees in these roles can work remotely while occasionally visiting facilities for on-site coordination.

In the legal and consulting professions, hybrid work models are increasingly common. Lawyers and consultants can handle documentation, research, and communication remotely, while client meetings and court appearances are conducted in person. Firms such as PwC and Deloitte have implemented flexible work policies to accommodate these variations.

The public sector has also adapted to hybrid models, particularly for administrative roles. Government agencies leverage digital platforms to provide services remotely, while retaining in-office operations for essential tasks. This approach ensures continuity of services while promoting employee well-being.

In conclusion, remote and hybrid work models manifest in various forms across industries, reflecting the specific demands and opportunities within each sector. By tailoring these models to their unique contexts, organizations can unlock the full potential of distributed work while addressing its inherent challenges.

3. The Future of Work

Emerging Trends in Distributed Work Models

Distributed work models have rapidly evolved, driven by advancements in technology, shifting workforce expectations, and external disruptions like the COVID-19 pandemic. As these models continue to mature, several key trends are shaping their future. These trends reflect the dynamic intersection of innovation, organizational strategy, and employee well-being.

1. Enhanced Digital Collaboration Platforms

The rise of distributed work has fueled demand for advanced digital collaboration tools. Basic video conferencing and chat applications are being augmented by AI-powered platforms that facilitate seamless interaction. Emerging tools integrate features such as real-time language translation, dynamic task prioritization, and predictive analytics to improve team efficiency.

Platforms like Microsoft Teams and Slack are evolving to become virtual ecosystems, supporting everything from project management to employee recognition programs. These tools aim to bridge gaps between remote and on-site workers, ensuring inclusivity and engagement in hybrid environments.

Looking ahead, augmented reality (AR) and virtual reality (VR) are poised to redefine virtual collaboration. These technologies will enable immersive experiences, such as virtual office spaces and 3D brainstorming sessions, offering a new dimension of interaction that mimics in-person dynamics.

2. Focus on Employee Experience (EX)

Organizations are increasingly prioritizing employee experience as a key factor in attracting and retaining talent. Distributed work models present unique opportunities to enhance EX by offering greater flexibility, personalized work environments, and access to global opportunities.

Companies are adopting measures such as flexible scheduling, well-being programs, and digital tools that empower employees to balance productivity with personal life. Customizable benefits, including access to coworking spaces or financial support for home office setups, are becoming standard.

The concept of "Work-Life Integration" is also gaining traction, replacing traditional notions of strict boundaries. By aligning organizational policies with individual preferences, businesses are fostering a sense of autonomy and satisfaction among their workforce.

3. Growth of Global Talent Pools

Distributed work models have dismantled geographical barriers, enabling organizations to tap into global talent pools. This trend allows companies to access diverse skill sets, reduce costs, and promote innovation through multicultural collaboration.

However, managing global teams requires careful consideration of cultural differences, legal compliance, and time zone challenges. To address these complexities, organizations are investing in technologies and frameworks that support asynchronous work, ensuring that all team members can contribute effectively despite location or time constraints.

The rise of borderless workforces has also led to an increase in "digital nomad" arrangements, where employees combine remote work with travel. Countries are responding by introducing digital nomad visas to attract skilled workers, further expanding opportunities for distributed work.

4. Emphasis on Sustainability

As environmental concerns become central to corporate strategies, distributed work models are emerging as a key component of sustainability initiatives. Remote work reduces commuting-related carbon emissions, while hybrid arrangements minimize the need for large office spaces, lowering energy consumption.

Organizations are adopting sustainable practices such as green office designs, energy-efficient technology, and paperless workflows. Employees working remotely are encouraged to adopt eco-friendly habits, supported by company policies that provide incentives for sustainable choices.

In the future, businesses will increasingly align their distributed work strategies with broader sustainability goals, leveraging technology to measure and reduce their environmental footprint.

5. Automation and AI Integration

Automation and artificial intelligence are transforming distributed work models by streamlining repetitive tasks and enhancing decision-making processes. AI-powered tools are used for everything from scheduling meetings to analyzing team performance, freeing employees to focus on high-value activities.

Chatbots and virtual assistants are becoming commonplace, providing instant support for employees working remotely. Predictive analytics tools help managers anticipate workload bottlenecks and allocate resources effectively, ensuring smooth operations across distributed teams.

In the coming years, AI will play a more significant role in enabling hyper-personalized employee experiences, automating routine processes, and fostering innovation through data-driven insights.

6. Decentralized Decision-Making

Distributed work models are driving a shift towards decentralized decision-making. Organizations are empowering teams to make decisions autonomously, reducing reliance on hierarchical structures. This approach not only improves agility but also fosters a sense of ownership and accountability among employees.

Decentralized decision-making is supported by transparent communication channels, real-time data access, and collaborative tools. As trust and empowerment become cornerstones of workplace culture, organizations are likely to see increased innovation and employee engagement.

7. Evolution of Leadership Styles

The rise of distributed work is reshaping leadership dynamics. Leaders are transitioning from traditional command-and-control approaches to more empathetic and facilitative roles. Skills such as active listening, emotional intelligence, and adaptability are becoming critical for managing remote and hybrid teams.

Future leaders will focus on fostering inclusive cultures, ensuring equitable access to opportunities, and promoting psychological safety. Training programs and leadership development initiatives will prioritize these competencies to prepare managers for the complexities of distributed work environments.

8. Redefining Office Spaces

The role of physical office spaces is changing in the era of distributed work. Rather than serving as the primary workplace, offices are evolving into hubs for collaboration, innovation, and community building.

Organizations are redesigning their offices to include flexible seating arrangements, breakout areas, and technology-equipped collaboration zones. These spaces are intended to complement remote work by providing opportunities for in-person interaction and team bonding.

As the trend towards flexible office spaces grows, businesses are also exploring shared or on-demand coworking arrangements to accommodate employees' diverse needs.

Predictions for Workplace Dynamics

1. Increased Flexibility as a Standard

Flexibility will become a non-negotiable aspect of workplace dynamics. Employees will expect the freedom to choose where, when, and how they work, based on their personal and professional needs. This shift will redefine traditional employment contracts and organizational policies, emphasizing results over rigid schedules.

Flexible work arrangements will also extend to compensation models, with companies offering customized packages that align with individual preferences and lifestyles.

2. Hybrid as the Dominant Model

Hybrid work is likely to emerge as the predominant model across industries. By balancing remote and in-office work, hybrid arrangements address the challenges of both extremes while maximizing their benefits. Organizations will continue to experiment with variations of the hybrid model to identify the most effective configurations for their workforce.

Successful hybrid strategies will prioritize inclusivity, ensuring that remote employees have equal access to resources, opportunities, and recognition.

3. Rise of the Four-Day Workweek

The four-day workweek is gaining traction as an innovative approach to enhancing productivity and well-being. By reducing the number of working days without compromising salaries, organizations aim to boost employee satisfaction and efficiency.

Early experiments with the four-day workweek have shown promising results, with employees reporting lower stress levels and higher engagement. As this trend gains momentum, it is likely to influence workplace dynamics in distributed environments.

4. Enhanced Focus on Mental Health

Mental health and well-being will remain central to workplace dynamics. Organizations will adopt proactive measures to support employees, including access to counseling services, wellness programs, and mental health training for leaders.

Flexible work arrangements will be complemented by initiatives that promote social interaction, reduce burnout, and encourage work-life harmony.

5. Integration of Advanced Technology

The workplace of the future will be defined by the integration of advanced technologies such as AI, blockchain, and the

Internet of Things (IoT). These innovations will enhance efficiency, security, and collaboration in distributed work models.

For example, blockchain can be used for secure document sharing, while IoT devices monitor and optimize home office environments. AI-driven insights will guide decision-making, ensuring that organizations stay ahead in a rapidly changing landscape.

6. Evolving Workplace Cultures

Workplace cultures will evolve to prioritize inclusivity, transparency, and innovation. Organizations will focus on building trust and fostering a sense of belonging, regardless of employees' locations.

Cultural alignment will be achieved through consistent communication, shared values, and opportunities for meaningful interaction. Leadership will play a crucial role in shaping and sustaining these cultures, ensuring that they adapt to the needs of a distributed workforce.

7. Global Standardization of Remote Work Policies

As remote and hybrid work become ubiquitous, governments and organizations will establish standardized policies to address legal, tax, and compliance issues. These frameworks will ensure fair treatment for employees and streamline processes for employers operating across borders.

In conclusion, the future of work is being shaped by emerging trends and evolving workplace dynamics. As organizations and employees navigate this transformative landscape, the focus will remain on leveraging technology, fostering inclusivity, and prioritizing well-being. By embracing these changes, businesses can create resilient and adaptive workforces equipped to thrive in an increasingly distributed world.

Part 2: Managing Distributed Teams

4. Building an Effective Distributed Team

Hiring for Remote and Hybrid Roles

Building a high-performing distributed team starts with hiring the right people. Recruiting for remote and hybrid roles presents unique challenges, but also offers significant advantages for organizations that take the time to refine their hiring practices. In this section, we will explore the key considerations when hiring for remote and hybrid positions and how organizations can adapt their recruitment strategies to ensure success.

1. Defining the Job and Expectations

The first step in hiring for remote and hybrid roles is to clearly define the job description and set expectations. Unlike traditional in-office roles, remote and hybrid positions require a different approach to job functions, especially when employees are spread across various locations and time zones.

Start by determining what skills and qualifications are essential for the role. Ensure that the responsibilities are realistic in the context of remote or hybrid work. For instance, roles that require heavy collaboration may benefit from hybrid setups where in-person meetings can supplement virtual interactions. Similarly, highly independent roles may be suited to fully remote work.

Remote and hybrid roles require clarity on communication protocols, working hours, and deliverables. Candidates need to understand the expectations for availability and response times, especially in hybrid environments where employees may not be online at the same time. By setting clear parameters from the beginning, businesses can reduce the risk of misunderstandings and frustrations.

2. Leveraging Technology for Recruitment

Recruiting for remote and hybrid roles demands the use of advanced technology to facilitate the hiring process. Traditional in-person interviews may no longer be viable, making it essential for companies to embrace virtual platforms that enable efficient recruitment. Tools such as video conferencing, skills assessment platforms, and AI-driven recruitment software can streamline the hiring process.

Video interviews allow hiring managers to assess candidates in real-time while observing non-verbal communication cues. Additionally, AI tools can assist with resume screening and candidate matching, helping recruiters identify individuals who best align with the needs of remote and hybrid roles.

Many platforms now offer simulations and real-world assessments designed to measure how candidates will perform in a remote or hybrid work environment. These tools can help determine whether the candidate is comfortable with the unique challenges of remote work, such as managing distractions or collaborating virtually.

3. Screening for Remote Competencies

When hiring for remote roles, it's essential to screen for competencies specific to working independently and managing time effectively. Remote work demands a high level of self-motivation, focus, and accountability. Recruiters need to assess whether candidates possess the soft skills and personal traits that align with remote work success.

Look for candidates who demonstrate a strong sense of ownership, excellent organizational skills, and proactive communication. It's essential to assess whether the candidate has the technological capabilities to perform their role effectively. A technical screening or an interview focusing on their experience with remote tools (e.g., Slack, Zoom, project management platforms) can be a good indicator of their ability to work effectively in a remote environment.

Assessing past remote work experience is also crucial. If the candidate has worked remotely before, they may already possess valuable insights on how to manage time zones, work independently, and communicate effectively in a digital environment.

4. Ensuring Cultural Fit and Alignment with Company Values

Cultural fit is a critical factor when hiring for remote and hybrid roles, as it helps ensure long-term engagement and satisfaction. Working remotely often requires more autonomy, and employees need to feel aligned with the company's values to remain motivated.

During the hiring process, assess how well candidates align with your company's culture. Ask questions related to their work style, how they handle challenges, and their preferred ways of communicating. Remote workers thrive in environments that prioritize trust, transparency, and communication. Understanding whether a candidate's values align with your organization's ethos can help improve retention rates and team cohesion.

It's also essential to consider how candidates may contribute to your organizational culture, even when working remotely. Are they likely to bring innovative ideas to the table? Do they value collaboration and inclusivity? These qualities can help build a team culture that transcends geographic boundaries.

5. Evaluating Communication Skills

Clear communication is the foundation of successful remote and hybrid teams. In the absence of face-to-face interactions, remote employees must be able to articulate their ideas effectively and work collaboratively across various communication channels.

When hiring for remote positions, assess a candidate's written and verbal communication skills. Do they clearly convey information in emails, instant messages, or video calls? How do they handle miscommunications or misunderstandings? Asking candidates to demonstrate their communication skills during the interview process is an effective way to gauge whether they'll succeed in a remote environment.

Proficiency in asynchronous communication is another important factor. In remote and hybrid teams, team members may be working in different time zones, making it essential for employees to communicate effectively without expecting instant responses. Candidates who are comfortable with asynchronous communication, such as leaving detailed feedback or updates for teammates in the form of recorded video or written reports, will likely thrive in a distributed team.

6. Onboarding Remote Employees Effectively

Once the right candidate is hired, onboarding becomes the next critical step in setting up remote employees for success. In a remote or hybrid work environment, onboarding must be comprehensive and structured to ensure new hires feel integrated into the team.

A robust remote onboarding process should include introductions to key team members, a clear overview of the organization's tools and resources, and an explanation of team dynamics. Virtual team-building activities can help create a sense of connection, while regular check-ins during the first few weeks ensure that the new hire feels supported.

Documentation is key to a successful remote onboarding process. Employees should have easy access to all relevant resources, from work guidelines to IT support. Clear documentation will also ensure that remote workers can independently resolve issues, fostering autonomy and reducing dependency on their manager for every step.

7. Ongoing Support and Development

The recruitment process doesn't end once an employee is hired; ongoing support and development are equally essential in managing remote and hybrid teams. Remote employees should have regular access to training, mentorship, and professional development opportunities to stay engaged and motivated.

Managers should also provide feedback that is constructive and tailored to the remote environment. Rather than in-person check-ins, remote employees may require feedback through digital platforms or scheduled video calls. Establishing a regular feedback loop will help employees feel valued and ensure that performance expectations are met.

Creating opportunities for social interaction, even in a remote setting, can improve team cohesion and morale. Virtual meetups, informal hangouts, and cross-department collaboration activities can foster relationships between remote workers, reducing the isolation often associated with distributed work.

Importance of Diversity and Inclusion in Distributed Teams

As remote and hybrid teams become the norm, diversity and inclusion (D&I) have emerged as central pillars of organizational success. A diverse workforce brings a variety of perspectives, experiences, and ideas, which are critical for fostering innovation and maintaining a competitive edge. For remote and hybrid teams, ensuring that diversity and inclusion are embedded in organizational practices is essential for creating an environment where all employees feel valued and supported.

1. The Business Case for Diversity and Inclusion

Research consistently shows that diverse teams are more innovative, productive, and effective. For remote and hybrid teams, diversity can drive creativity and problem-solving by offering a range of viewpoints and experiences. When employees from different backgrounds collaborate, they bring unique solutions to the table, which can lead to more effective decision-making and better business outcomes.

Inclusion, on the other hand, ensures that all employees—regardless of background—have equal access to opportunities and resources. This is particularly important in remote and hybrid teams, where employees may feel disconnected or isolated from the rest of the organization.

Inclusive practices also foster employee satisfaction and retention. When employees feel like they belong and are valued for who they are, they are more likely to stay with the company long-term, reducing turnover costs and enhancing team stability.

2. Building Diverse Teams in a Remote Environment

Building diverse teams in a remote setting requires intentionality and strategic action. Start by ensuring that recruitment processes are inclusive and that hiring managers are trained to recognize unconscious biases. Additionally, making use of global talent pools, which are a major benefit of distributed teams, is an excellent way to bring in diverse perspectives.

When hiring remotely, consider applicants from different geographical locations, cultures, and backgrounds. For hybrid teams, it's important to make sure that employees from various backgrounds feel equally included, whether they work in the office or remotely.

3. Addressing Bias in Distributed Teams

In distributed teams, bias can often be more difficult to identify and address, as remote employees may not have the same visibility or opportunities for in-person interaction. Bias can manifest in several ways, such as unequal access to career development, fewer opportunities to contribute in team meetings, or being excluded from informal social interactions.

Organizations need to actively monitor and address bias in their remote and hybrid teams. This can be achieved by setting clear policies on inclusion, offering bias training, and ensuring that all employees are given equal opportunities to thrive.

Additionally, using technology to track participation in meetings, contributions to projects, and engagement levels can help identify areas where bias may be creeping in. Regular audits of team dynamics and feedback from employees can uncover issues early, allowing organizations to correct them promptly.

4. Inclusive Communication Practices

Effective communication is crucial in remote and hybrid teams, but it must also be inclusive. Not all team members have the same communication style, and some employees may face challenges such as language barriers, different time zones, or access to technology.

It's essential for teams to establish clear communication guidelines that promote inclusivity. This may include providing translated materials, using accessible communication tools, or adopting asynchronous communication to accommodate varying time zones.

Encouraging open feedback and creating channels for underrepresented voices to be heard are also key to fostering an inclusive environment. Managers should

5. Fostering a Culture of Belonging

For distributed teams to succeed, employees must feel that they are an integral part of the organization, regardless of their physical location. Fostering a sense of belonging is essential to create a cohesive and motivated team.

Managers play a critical role in promoting belonging by ensuring that remote and hybrid employees are treated equitably and included in team activities. This might involve celebrating cultural diversity within the team, acknowledging and respecting religious or cultural holidays, and incorporating inclusive practices into everyday operations.

Virtual team-building exercises and consistent recognition of individual and group achievements can also strengthen the feeling of being part of a community. Employees who feel valued are more likely to stay engaged, contributing positively to team dynamics and overall organizational success.

6. Providing Equal Access to Resources and Opportunities

One of the primary challenges in managing distributed teams is ensuring that all employees have equal access to the tools, resources, and opportunities they need to thrive. Remote employees, especially those in different geographical regions, may face disparities in technology access, mentorship, or career advancement.

To address these disparities, organizations must invest in the infrastructure needed to support remote employees effectively. This includes providing the necessary hardware and software, offering flexible schedules to accommodate time zone differences, and ensuring access to learning and development programs.

Additionally, career growth opportunities must be made equally accessible to all team members, regardless of their physical location. This can be achieved by establishing transparent promotion criteria and ensuring that remote employees are considered for leadership roles and special projects.

7. Measuring Diversity and Inclusion in Distributed Teams

To ensure the success of diversity and inclusion initiatives, organizations need to regularly measure their effectiveness. Metrics such as employee satisfaction, turnover rates, and the diversity of new hires can provide valuable insights into how well the organization is doing in building an inclusive culture.

Conducting anonymous surveys can help identify areas where remote employees may feel excluded or unsupported. Regularly reviewing team composition, participation levels in meetings, and access to resources can also highlight gaps in inclusivity.

Using this data, organizations can refine their policies and practices to create a truly inclusive environment that supports the needs of all employees, regardless of where they work.

Building an effective distributed team requires a combination of strategic hiring, fostering diversity and inclusion, and ensuring that all employees have equal opportunities to succeed. By prioritizing these elements, organizations can create a thriving distributed workforce that is not only productive but also innovative and resilient.

As remote and hybrid work continues to evolve, the ability to manage distributed teams effectively will become a core competency for organizations looking to stay competitive in a global market. With the right approach, distributed teams can achieve remarkable results while fostering a culture of inclusivity and belonging.

5. Leadership Strategies for Distributed Teams

Adapting Leadership Styles for Remote Management

Leadership in distributed teams differs significantly from traditional in-office management. In a remote or hybrid setting, leaders must adapt their styles to accommodate new challenges, including physical distance, varying time zones, and reliance on digital communication. This section explores the key strategies for adapting leadership styles to ensure effective team management and cohesion.

1. Understanding the Remote Leadership Paradigm

Remote leadership requires a shift from a command-and-control approach to one that emphasizes trust, communication, and empowerment. Leaders must focus on guiding outcomes rather than micromanaging daily tasks. With team members working independently, fostering a sense of ownership and accountability becomes a priority.

Effective remote leadership hinges on clear communication, as physical absence can lead to misunderstandings. Leaders need to prioritize proactive and transparent communication, ensuring that their team members understand expectations, deadlines, and goals. Additionally, building rapport through regular check-ins and virtual meetings helps bridge the gap created by the lack of in-person interactions.

2. Prioritizing Emotional Intelligence

In a remote environment, emotional intelligence (EI) is a critical skill for leaders. Understanding and managing one's emotions, as well as recognizing and addressing the emotions of others, becomes even more important when team members are dispersed. Leaders with high EI can sense when employees are struggling with challenges such as isolation, burnout, or miscommunication.

For example, a leader might notice decreased participation in meetings or a shift in tone in email communications. Addressing these issues promptly, with empathy and understanding, can help maintain morale and prevent disengagement. Virtual one-on-one meetings offer an opportunity to provide support and foster a sense of connection.

3. Emphasizing Flexibility and Adaptability

Remote and hybrid teams often operate across different time zones and schedules, requiring leaders to adopt a flexible approach. Unlike traditional office environments, where employees are present during fixed hours, distributed teams may need to work asynchronously.

Leaders should focus on outcomes rather than hours worked. By setting clear goals and allowing employees the autonomy to determine how they achieve them, leaders empower their teams while accommodating individual work styles. This flexibility can enhance productivity and employee satisfaction.

Adapting to the needs of individual team members is also critical. For example, some employees may prefer video calls for collaboration, while others excel with written communication. Leaders must be adaptable in their communication methods, ensuring that all team members feel comfortable and included.

4. Leveraging Technology for Leadership

Technology plays a pivotal role in remote leadership. Leaders must become proficient in using digital tools for communication, collaboration, and performance management. Platforms like Zoom, Microsoft Teams, Slack, and project management software such as Trello or Asana enable leaders to stay connected with their teams and track progress effectively.

Regular use of these tools can help leaders maintain visibility into their teams' activities without resorting to micromanagement. However, leaders must also be mindful of not overwhelming employees with excessive virtual meetings or constant notifications. Striking a balance is key to maintaining productivity and focus.

Leaders should also use technology to celebrate achievements and recognize individual and team contributions. Virtual shoutouts, digital awards, or even a dedicated channel for celebrating milestones can boost morale and foster a sense of community.

5. Leading with Clarity and Vision

Distributed teams often face challenges in aligning with organizational goals due to the lack of face-to-face interactions. Leaders must articulate a clear vision and mission for their teams, ensuring that every member understands how their role contributes to the organization's success.

A strong sense of purpose can motivate remote employees and create a sense of unity. Leaders should frequently reiterate goals during team meetings and provide updates on progress to keep everyone aligned. Visual aids, such as dashboards or shared documents, can help track milestones and keep the team focused on priorities.

6. Encouraging Collaboration and Innovation

Collaboration in distributed teams requires deliberate effort. Leaders must create an environment that encourages team members to share ideas, contribute to discussions, and innovate. This involves setting up platforms and processes that facilitate collaboration, such as brainstorming sessions, shared workspaces, or innovation challenges.

Virtual meetings should be structured to encourage participation, with clear agendas and opportunities for everyone to contribute. Leaders can also pair team members for projects, fostering peer collaboration and building stronger interpersonal connections within the team.

Encouraging diversity of thought is another crucial aspect. By valuing the unique perspectives of team members from different backgrounds, leaders can drive innovation and problem-solving.

7. Developing Leadership Presence in a Virtual World

Building a strong leadership presence is more challenging in a virtual environment but equally important. Leaders must be visible, approachable, and engaged with their teams. Regular virtual town halls, office hours, and team check-ins can help establish this presence.

Non-verbal communication, such as body language and tone of voice, plays a critical role in virtual interactions. Leaders should be mindful of their virtual demeanor, ensuring that they appear attentive and engaged during video calls. Consistency in communication and follow-through on commitments further reinforces a leader's credibility and presence.

Creating Accountability and Trust

Accountability and trust are foundational elements of successful distributed teams. Without the daily oversight of traditional office environments, leaders must implement strategies to foster a culture of accountability while building trust among team members.

1. Establishing Clear Goals and Expectations

Accountability begins with clarity. Leaders must set clear, measurable goals for their teams, ensuring that every member understands their individual responsibilities. SMART (Specific, Measurable, Achievable, Relevant, Time-bound) goals provide a framework for defining and tracking objectives.

Regularly revisiting these goals and updating progress ensures that everyone remains aligned. Clear expectations regarding deadlines, quality standards, and communication protocols also reduce ambiguity and promote accountability.

2. Building a Culture of Ownership

In distributed teams, employees must take ownership of their work. Leaders can foster this culture by empowering team members to make decisions and take initiative. Providing autonomy and recognizing achievements helps employees feel a sense of pride and responsibility for their contributions.

Encouraging team members to share updates on their progress during meetings or through project management tools also reinforces accountability. Peer accountability can be particularly effective, as team members are more likely to stay committed when they know their colleagues depend on them.

3. Encouraging Open and Transparent Communication

Trust thrives in an environment of transparency. Leaders should encourage open communication within their teams, where employees feel comfortable discussing challenges, seeking feedback, and sharing ideas.

Transparency from leadership is equally important. Regular updates on organizational priorities, decisions, and challenges build trust and demonstrate that the leader values honesty and collaboration.

Providing feedback in a constructive and supportive manner is another way to build trust. Employees need to feel that their efforts are recognized and that they are supported in overcoming obstacles.

4. Monitoring Without Micromanaging

Leaders must strike a balance between monitoring performance and giving employees the freedom to work independently. Micromanagement can erode trust and stifle creativity, while too little oversight can lead to missed deadlines or subpar performance.

Using technology to track progress without being intrusive is key. For example, project management tools can provide visibility into task completion and timelines without requiring constant check-ins.

Periodic performance reviews and one-on-one meetings can help leaders stay informed about individual progress while providing an opportunity to address concerns and offer support.

5. Promoting Team Accountability

Accountability is not solely the responsibility of the leader. Encouraging team accountability creates a sense of collective responsibility and strengthens collaboration. Team members who hold each other accountable are more likely to remain committed to shared goals.

Leaders can facilitate this by promoting open discussions about progress, celebrating team achievements, and addressing challenges collectively. Encouraging peer feedback and support fosters a sense of unity and shared purpose.

6. Building and Maintaining Trust

Trust is the cornerstone of successful distributed teams. Leaders must actively build trust by demonstrating integrity, consistency, and reliability. Following through on commitments, being transparent about decisions, and treating all team members equitably are essential to establishing trust.

Creating opportunities for informal interactions, such as virtual coffee chats or team-building activities, can also strengthen relationships and build trust among team members.

Trust-building is an ongoing process, requiring consistent effort from leaders to create an environment where employees feel valued, respected, and supported.

By adapting leadership styles and focusing on accountability and trust, leaders can successfully manage distributed teams, driving performance and fostering a positive team culture in remote and hybrid environments.

6. Communication and Engagement

Managing Communication Across Time Zones

Effective communication is the backbone of distributed teams, and managing it across time zones requires thoughtful strategies to ensure all team members feel connected and informed. Time zone differences can create challenges in collaboration, delay decision-making, and lead to misalignment if not handled effectively.

1. Understanding the Impact of Time Zone Differences

Distributed teams often span multiple time zones, which can lead to gaps in communication. Employees working in different regions may face delays in receiving updates or responses to their queries, which can hinder productivity and morale.

These challenges are further amplified when tasks require real-time collaboration or urgent decision-making. For example, a team member in Asia may need input from a colleague in North America, leading to an unavoidable 12-hour delay. Leaders must recognize these challenges and implement strategies to bridge the gaps.

2. Creating a Time Zone-Friendly Communication Framework

To ensure seamless communication, leaders should create a framework that accounts for time zone differences. This includes:

Identifying Overlapping Work Hours: Determine periods during the day when all team members can be available for synchronous communication. Tools like Google Calendar's world clock or scheduling assistants can help identify suitable meeting times.

Using Asynchronous Communication Tools: Platforms like Slack, Microsoft Teams, or email can facilitate communication that doesn't require immediate responses. Leaders should encourage the use of asynchronous tools for non-urgent matters.

Setting Response Expectations: Clearly communicate acceptable response times for different types of communication. For example, emails may have a 24-hour response window, while urgent messages require same-day replies.

3. Implementing "Follow-the-Sun" Models for Collaboration

A "follow-the-sun" model, where tasks are handed off across time zones to ensure continuous progress, is an effective way to leverage distributed teams. For example, a design team in Europe can begin a project that a team in the Americas continues during their working hours, and then it moves to a team in Asia for further work.

This model requires clear documentation and smooth transitions. Leaders should ensure that team members leave detailed updates at the end of their shifts, enabling their counterparts to pick up where they left off without confusion.

4. Leveraging Technology to Bridge Time Zones

Technology plays a vital role in managing communication across time zones. Cloud-based tools like Google Drive,

Dropbox, and Notion allow team members to collaborate on documents and projects in real time or asynchronously.

Automated notifications can remind team members about upcoming deadlines or meetings, while shared calendars enable everyone to stay aligned on schedules. Tools like Loom can be used to record video updates for team members in different time zones, adding a personal touch to asynchronous communication.

5. Addressing Cultural and Linguistic Barriers

Time zone management often intersects with cultural and linguistic diversity. Leaders must be sensitive to cultural differences that may influence communication preferences and work styles. For instance, some cultures may prefer direct communication, while others value subtlety.

Encouraging the use of a shared language for all work-related communication and providing access to language support tools, such as translation software, can help mitigate misunderstandings. Training sessions on cross-cultural communication can further enhance collaboration.

6. Building Awareness and Empathy

A distributed team thrives when its members understand and empathize with the challenges their colleagues face in different time zones. Leaders can promote this by:

Encouraging team members to respect boundaries, such as avoiding sending messages outside of someone's working hours.

Rotating meeting times to distribute the inconvenience of early or late calls across the team.

Providing flexibility for team members to adjust their schedules when attending critical meetings outside of their normal working hours.

By fostering awareness and empathy, leaders can create a collaborative environment where all team members feel valued and supported.

Best Practices for Virtual Meetings and Check-Ins

Virtual meetings and check-ins are essential for maintaining communication and building relationships in distributed teams. However, without proper planning, they can become inefficient and disengaging.

1. Structuring Virtual Meetings for Success

Virtual meetings should be purposeful and well-structured to maximize productivity. Best practices include:

Setting Clear Objectives: Before scheduling a meeting, ensure that it has a clear purpose. Communicate the agenda to participants in advance so they can come prepared.

Limiting Participants: Invite only those who are directly involved or impacted by the topics discussed to avoid unnecessary disruptions.

Sticking to Timelines: Start and end meetings on time to respect everyone's schedules. Time zone differences should be factored into meeting duration.

Using Collaborative Tools: Platforms like Zoom, Microsoft Teams, and Miro can enhance engagement by allowing participants to share screens, annotate documents, or brainstorm ideas.

2. Encouraging Participation and Engagement

Virtual meetings can often feel impersonal, leading to disengagement. Leaders can foster active participation by:

Inviting input from every participant, ensuring quieter team members have a chance to speak.

Using breakout rooms for smaller group discussions, which can encourage collaboration and interaction.

Incorporating interactive elements, such as polls, Q&A sessions, or icebreakers, to make meetings more engaging.

3. Scheduling Regular Check-Ins

Frequent one-on-one and team check-ins are vital for keeping remote employees connected and aligned. These check-ins should focus on:

Reviewing progress on tasks and addressing roadblocks.

Discussing career development goals and providing feedback.

Offering support for personal and professional challenges.

Leaders should adapt their frequency and format based on individual team members' needs.

4. Recording and Sharing Meeting Summaries

To ensure inclusivity and continuity, meetings should be recorded, and key takeaways shared with all team members, especially those who couldn't attend. Summaries should highlight action items, deadlines, and decisions made.

Strategies for Boosting Employee Engagement

Maintaining high levels of employee engagement is challenging in distributed teams, where isolation and disengagement can easily set in. Proactive strategies can help leaders foster a motivated and connected team.

1. Recognizing and Celebrating Achievements

Recognition is a powerful motivator. Leaders should celebrate individual and team accomplishments through virtual shoutouts, awards, or team emails. Personalizing recognition, such as highlighting specific contributions, can make it more meaningful.

2. Encouraging Professional Growth

Engaged employees are those who see opportunities for growth and development. Leaders can:

Provide access to online learning platforms and courses.

Support attendance at virtual conferences or webinars.

Assign challenging projects that enable employees to expand their skill sets.

3. Organizing Virtual Team-Building Activities

Team-building fosters camaraderie and a sense of belonging. Virtual activities like trivia games, cooking classes, or fitness challenges can help bring distributed teams closer.

4. Promoting Work-Life Balance

Employee engagement is closely tied to well-being. Leaders can support work-life balance by:

Encouraging regular breaks and time off.

Setting boundaries for work communication outside of hours.

Providing wellness resources, such as access to meditation apps or virtual fitness sessions.

5. Gathering Feedback and Acting on It

Regularly soliciting feedback from employees demonstrates that their opinions are valued. Leaders should conduct surveys or hold open forums to understand challenges and suggestions for improvement.

Acting on feedback quickly and transparently builds trust and shows commitment to employee satisfaction.

By mastering communication across time zones, optimizing virtual meetings, and implementing engagement strategies, leaders can ensure that their distributed teams remain productive, motivated, and connected. The success of these initiatives ultimately depends on consistent effort, adaptability, and a commitment to supporting the team's well-being.

7. Performance Management in Remote Settings

Managing performance in remote work environments is both a challenge and an opportunity for modern organizations. Unlike traditional settings where direct supervision is possible, remote work requires redefining how expectations are set, performance is evaluated, and success is measured. Leaders must adopt new approaches that are transparent, data-driven, and adaptable to the unique dynamics of distributed teams.

Setting Clear Expectations and Goals

One of the most critical aspects of performance management in remote settings is establishing clarity around expectations and goals. Without physical proximity, ambiguity in roles or tasks can lead to confusion, inefficiencies, and dissatisfaction.

1. The Importance of Clear Expectations in Remote Work

In traditional office environments, employees often rely on informal cues, face-to-face discussions, or in-the-moment guidance to understand expectations. However, in remote settings, these opportunities are limited. Clear expectations serve as a roadmap, ensuring that employees know what is required of them, how their work contributes to organizational goals, and the standards by which they will be assessed.

When expectations are poorly defined, employees may:

Struggle to prioritize tasks.

Misinterpret their roles.

Experience stress due to uncertainty.

2. Establishing Well-Defined Goals

Setting goals in a remote environment requires specificity and alignment with broader organizational objectives. The SMART framework—goals that are Specific, Measurable, Achievable, Relevant, and Time-bound—is particularly effective for remote teams.

For example:

Specific: Replace vague goals like "improve customer satisfaction" with detailed ones like "reduce customer response time by 20% over the next quarter."

Measurable: Define metrics to track progress, such as customer satisfaction scores or ticket resolution times.

Achievable: Ensure goals are realistic given the resources and time available.

Relevant: Align goals with team or organizational priorities.

Time-bound: Set deadlines to create a sense of urgency and focus.

3. Communicating Expectations Effectively

Once expectations are defined, communicating them effectively is essential. Leaders should:

Use written documentation: Share detailed job descriptions, task guidelines, or project charters through shared platforms like Google Docs or Notion.

Conduct regular one-on-one meetings: These discussions provide an opportunity to clarify roles, address questions, and ensure alignment.

Record expectations: In team meetings or goal-setting sessions, ensure that expectations are documented and accessible to all stakeholders.

Transparency in communication reduces misunderstandings and empowers employees to take ownership of their responsibilities.

4. Providing Continuous Feedback

Setting expectations is not a one-time activity—it requires ongoing feedback to ensure alignment and adaptation. Regular feedback loops help employees understand how they are performing relative to expectations and identify areas for improvement.

Effective feedback includes:

Real-time insights: Use tools like Slack or Microsoft Teams to provide quick feedback on specific tasks.

Structured reviews: Schedule bi-weekly or monthly check-ins to discuss performance, challenges, and progress toward goals.

Balanced approach: Offer constructive criticism alongside recognition of achievements to maintain morale.

5. Setting Expectations Around Communication and Availability

Remote teams often operate in different time zones, making it essential to establish expectations for availability and response times. Leaders can:

Define "core hours" for synchronous collaboration.

Encourage the use of asynchronous tools for non-urgent communication.

Specify acceptable response times for emails or messages, such as within 24 hours.

By setting these expectations upfront, leaders can prevent misunderstandings and ensure smooth workflows.

Measuring and Evaluating Team Performance

Evaluating performance in remote settings presents unique challenges. Traditional metrics such as attendance or visibility are no longer relevant, requiring leaders to adopt more outcome-focused approaches.

1. Shifting from Input-Based to Output-Based Metrics

In remote work environments, productivity cannot be measured by the number of hours an employee spends online. Instead, leaders should focus on output-based metrics, such as:

Deliverables completed within deadlines.

Quality of work produced.

Achievement of individual and team goals.

For example, a content writer's performance might be assessed based on the number of articles written, their adherence to style guidelines, and audience engagement metrics.

2. Leveraging Key Performance Indicators (KPIs)

Key Performance Indicators (KPIs) provide a quantifiable way to measure success. Remote teams should have KPIs tailored to their roles and responsibilities, such as:

Sales teams: Revenue generated, number of leads converted.

Customer support teams: Average resolution time, customer satisfaction scores.

Development teams: Number of features released, bug resolution rates.

KPIs should be reviewed regularly to ensure they remain relevant and achievable.

3. Utilizing Technology for Performance Tracking

Technology plays a vital role in tracking performance in remote settings. Tools like Trello, Asana, and Monday.com enable teams to manage tasks, track progress, and monitor deadlines. For instance:

Project management platforms: Provide visibility into task statuses and deadlines.

Analytics tools: Offer insights into team performance metrics, such as sales figures or website traffic.

Employee engagement software: Helps track employee sentiment and identify potential issues.

4. Conducting Performance Reviews

Performance reviews are an opportunity to evaluate accomplishments, discuss challenges, and set future goals. In remote settings, these reviews should be:

Data-driven: Use objective metrics and examples to support evaluations.

Collaborative: Involve employees in self-assessments to gain their perspective.

Forward-looking: Focus on growth opportunities and development plans rather than solely reviewing past performance.

Regular performance reviews, conducted quarterly or bi-annually, help maintain alignment and provide employees with a sense of direction.

5. Balancing Individual and Team Metrics

While individual performance metrics are important, leaders should also measure team dynamics. Strong collaboration and team cohesion are essential for distributed teams to succeed. Metrics such as team productivity, peer feedback, and collective goal achievement can provide insights into overall team health.

6. Addressing Underperformance

When performance issues arise, addressing them promptly and constructively is critical. Leaders should:

Identify root causes: Determine whether underperformance is due to a lack of clarity, resources, or personal challenges.

Offer support: Provide additional training, mentorship, or tools to help employees improve.

Set improvement plans: Define clear steps and timelines for addressing performance gaps.

Approaching underperformance with empathy and a solutions-oriented mindset fosters trust and motivates employees to improve.

7. Recognizing and Rewarding Excellence

Recognition is a powerful motivator, especially in remote settings where employees may feel isolated. Leaders should celebrate achievements through:

Virtual shoutouts during team meetings.

Personalized messages of appreciation.

Monetary or non-monetary rewards, such as bonuses or gift cards.

Recognition reinforces positive behavior and creates a culture of appreciation.

8. Continuous Improvement and Adaptation

Performance management is an ongoing process that requires regular evaluation and adaptation. Leaders should solicit feedback from employees on the effectiveness of performance management practices and make adjustments as needed.

For example:

If employees find KPIs too rigid, involve them in redefining metrics that better align with their roles.

If communication gaps persist, explore new tools or processes to enhance clarity.

By continuously refining performance management strategies, organizations can ensure that their remote teams remain productive, engaged, and aligned with organizational goals.

Through clear goal-setting, thoughtful evaluation, and proactive support, leaders can effectively manage performance in remote settings. These practices not only drive individual and team success but also foster a culture of accountability, trust, and excellence in distributed work environments.

Part 3: Technology and Collaboration Tools

8. Choosing the Right Tools

In the era of remote and hybrid work, the tools an organization chooses can determine the efficiency, collaboration, and overall success of its distributed teams. These tools not only facilitate communication but also play a crucial role in task management, resource allocation, and building a cohesive team culture across distances. The right combination of tools tailored to an organization's needs can significantly streamline workflows, reduce misunderstandings, and enhance productivity.

Overview of Popular Collaboration and Communication Platforms

1. The Role of Collaboration Platforms in Distributed Work

Collaboration platforms act as the backbone of communication and coordination in remote settings. These platforms help teams stay connected, share updates in real-time, and ensure that work progresses smoothly regardless of geographical boundaries. Popular collaboration tools have evolved to incorporate features like file sharing, video conferencing, project management, and integrations with other software.

2. Popular Collaboration Platforms

Slack:

Slack is one of the most widely used platforms for real-time communication. Its channels enable team-specific discussions, while integrations with tools like Google Drive, Trello, and Zoom make it a versatile option. Slack also supports asynchronous communication through features like reminders and message scheduling, catering to distributed teams operating across time zones.

Microsoft Teams:

Microsoft Teams combines video conferencing, chat, and file sharing into a single platform. Its deep integration with Microsoft 365 products like Word, Excel, and SharePoint makes it particularly suitable for organizations already using the Microsoft ecosystem. Teams also offers robust security features, making it a popular choice for industries like finance and healthcare.

Zoom:

Known for its simplicity and reliability, Zoom is the go-to platform for virtual meetings. Its breakout rooms, screen-sharing capabilities, and webinar hosting features make it suitable for both internal team meetings and external client interactions. Zoom also supports integrations with numerous productivity tools, enhancing its functionality.

Asana and Trello:

These project management tools focus on task tracking and team collaboration. Asana provides a structured framework for planning, while Trello's card-based interface offers flexibility for creative workflows. Both platforms help teams visualize progress, assign responsibilities, and meet deadlines efficiently.

Google Workspace:

Google Workspace combines communication (Gmail, Chat, and Meet) with productivity tools (Docs, Sheets, and Slides). Its cloud-based infrastructure enables real-time collaboration, allowing teams to co-edit documents and track changes seamlessly.

3. Specialized Tools for Collaboration

In addition to general collaboration platforms, specialized tools cater to specific needs:

Miro and MURAL: Digital whiteboards for brainstorming and collaborative ideation sessions.

Notion: A versatile knowledge management tool that combines note-taking, databases, and project management.

Figma: A design collaboration platform for teams working on UI/UX or graphic design projects.

Key Features to Look for in Collaboration Tools

When selecting collaboration tools, organizations should prioritize:

Ease of Use: Tools should have an intuitive interface to minimize onboarding time and encourage widespread adoption.

Scalability: Platforms should accommodate the growing needs of the organization, whether in terms of user capacity or feature expansion.

Security: Robust encryption, compliance with data privacy regulations, and user access controls are critical for protecting sensitive information.

Integration Capabilities: Tools that integrate seamlessly with other software in the organization's tech stack enable smoother workflows.

Customization Options: Flexibility to adapt tools to specific workflows or branding requirements adds value.

Integration of Tools for Seamless Workflows

1. The Need for Integrated Workflows

Remote work often involves juggling multiple platforms for communication, task management, and documentation. Without integration, teams risk inefficiencies such as duplicated efforts, lost information, and delayed responses. Integrated workflows eliminate these challenges by creating a unified system where tools communicate with one another.

2. Benefits of Integration

Streamlined Processes: Automation of repetitive tasks, such as updating task statuses or notifying team members about changes.

Centralized Data: Consolidation of information across platforms reduces the risk of data silos.

Improved Collaboration: Real-time syncing of updates ensures that all team members are on the same page.

Enhanced Productivity: Teams can focus on their core tasks instead of toggling between multiple tools.

3. Common Integration Scenarios

Email and Project Management:

Integrating tools like Gmail with Asana allows users to convert emails into tasks directly from their inbox. This ensures that important communication doesn't fall through the cracks.

Chat and File Sharing:

Platforms like Slack integrate with Google Drive and OneDrive, enabling team members to share, access, and edit documents without leaving the chat interface.

Video Conferencing and Calendar Management:

Tools like Zoom or Microsoft Teams sync with Google Calendar or Outlook, making it easy to schedule and join meetings.

CRM and Collaboration Tools:

Customer Relationship Management (CRM) software like Salesforce integrates with platforms like Trello, enabling sales teams to track customer interactions and manage deals effectively.

Automation Tools:

Platforms like Zapier or Make act as intermediaries that connect disparate tools, automating workflows without requiring custom coding. For example, a trigger in Trello (e.g., moving a card to "Completed") can automatically send a notification via Slack.

4. Strategies for Successful Integration

To maximize the benefits of integration, organizations should:

Map Existing Workflows: Identify pain points and redundancies in current processes to determine where integration can add value.

Choose Compatible Tools: Ensure that selected tools support the necessary APIs or pre-built integrations.

Standardize Processes: Define clear guidelines for how tools will be used to prevent confusion and inconsistency.

Train Employees: Provide training sessions or documentation to help teams navigate the integrated environment effectively.

Monitor and Adjust: Regularly assess the effectiveness of integrations and make adjustments as needed to address evolving requirements.

5. Challenges of Integration and How to Overcome Them

Despite its advantages, integrating tools can pose challenges:

Complexity: Managing multiple integrations can become overwhelming. Solution: Use centralized platforms like Slack or Microsoft Teams to minimize fragmentation.

Cost: Premium features or advanced integrations often come at a cost. Solution: Prioritize high-impact integrations that deliver measurable ROI.

Resistance to Change: Employees may be hesitant to adopt new workflows. Solution: Involve team members in the decision-making process and highlight the benefits of integration.

6. The Future of Tool Integration

As remote and hybrid work continues to evolve, the emphasis on integration will grow. Emerging technologies like artificial intelligence (AI) and machine learning (ML) will further enhance tool integration by enabling predictive analytics, intelligent automation, and personalized user experiences.

AI-Driven Insights: Tools will analyze workflows and recommend optimizations based on usage patterns.

Cross-Platform Interoperability: Advances in interoperability standards will make it easier for tools from different vendors to work together seamlessly.

Unified Dashboards: Centralized dashboards that aggregate data and insights from multiple tools will become the norm, simplifying decision-making for managers and employees alike.

By carefully selecting and integrating collaboration tools, organizations can create an environment where distributed teams thrive. The right tools not only enhance productivity but also foster a sense of connection and alignment, even in the absence of physical proximity.

9. Ensuring Secure and Efficient Communication

The transition to remote and hybrid work has brought unparalleled flexibility and productivity benefits but also introduced new challenges, especially in communication security. Distributed teams rely heavily on digital channels for communication and collaboration, making robust cybersecurity measures and data protection strategies essential to safeguarding organizational assets and ensuring compliance with regulatory standards. This chapter delves into the intricacies of cybersecurity considerations for distributed work and explores data protection and privacy strategies to enable secure and efficient communication in remote and hybrid environments.

Cybersecurity Considerations for Distributed Work

1. Understanding the Cybersecurity Landscape in Distributed Work

The rise of remote and hybrid work models has significantly expanded the attack surface for cyber threats. Employees working from various locations and networks create vulnerabilities that cybercriminals can exploit. Threats like phishing, ransomware, data breaches, and insider threats have become more prevalent, targeting not just individuals but entire organizations.

Increased Dependency on Digital Tools: The reliance on cloud-based platforms, video conferencing, and collaboration tools has made secure communication a cornerstone of distributed work.

Use of Personal Devices: Many employees use their personal laptops and smartphones for work-related tasks, introducing risks associated with unsecured devices and networks.

2. Implementing Secure Communication Protocols

To mitigate risks, organizations must implement robust security measures:

End-to-End Encryption: Communication platforms like Microsoft Teams, Slack, and Zoom must use end-to-end encryption to ensure that messages, calls, and files are accessible only to intended recipients.

Multi-Factor Authentication (MFA): MFA adds an extra layer of security by requiring users to verify their identity using two or more methods, such as passwords, biometrics, or one-time codes.

Virtual Private Networks (VPNs): VPNs encrypt internet connections, protecting sensitive data transmitted over public or home networks. Organizations should provide employees with secure VPNs for accessing company resources.

Regular Software Updates: Outdated software can be a gateway for cyberattacks. Organizations must enforce regular updates for all applications and operating systems used by employees.

3. Educating Employees About Cybersecurity

The human factor is often the weakest link in cybersecurity. Comprehensive training programs can empower employees to recognize and respond to threats:

Phishing Awareness: Simulated phishing campaigns can help employees identify fraudulent emails, links, and attachments.

Password Hygiene: Encourage the use of strong, unique passwords and password managers to avoid reuse across multiple accounts.

Incident Reporting: Create a culture where employees feel comfortable reporting suspected security breaches without fear of repercussions.

4. Securing Collaboration and Communication Tools

The platforms employees use daily must adhere to stringent security standards:

Access Control: Implement role-based access controls (RBAC) to restrict access to sensitive information based on employees' roles.

Audit Logs: Enable logging and monitoring features to track user activities and detect anomalies in real-time.

Third-Party Integrations: Vet third-party applications integrated with communication tools to ensure they meet security and compliance requirements.

5. Managing Remote Endpoint Security

Each device connected to the company network represents a potential entry point for cyber threats. Endpoint security involves safeguarding these devices through:

Endpoint Detection and Response (EDR): EDR solutions provide continuous monitoring and detection of threats on endpoints.

Mobile Device Management (MDM): MDM software ensures that mobile devices comply with organizational security policies and allows remote wiping of data in case of loss or theft.

Secure Configurations: Mandate the use of firewalls, antivirus software, and disk encryption on all employee devices.

6. Responding to Security Incidents

Despite preventive measures, breaches may still occur. A well-defined incident response plan can minimize damage:

Incident Response Teams: Establish teams responsible for managing and mitigating security incidents.

Communication Protocols: Define how and when employees should report suspected breaches and how the organization will communicate updates.

Post-Incident Reviews: Analyze the root cause of incidents to improve future defenses.

Data Protection and Privacy

1. The Importance of Data Protection in Distributed Work

Remote work increases the volume of data shared over digital platforms, heightening the need for robust data protection practices. Organizations must comply with regulations such as the General Data Protection Regulation (GDPR), California Consumer Privacy Act (CCPA), and others to avoid legal and reputational risks.

2. Establishing Data Protection Policies

Clear policies provide a framework for handling sensitive information:

Data Classification: Categorize data based on sensitivity levels (e.g., public, internal, confidential) and apply appropriate safeguards for each category.

Data Minimization: Collect only the data necessary for business operations to reduce exposure to risks.

Retention Policies: Define how long data will be stored and establish procedures for secure disposal of obsolete information.

3. Encrypting Sensitive Data

Encryption transforms data into unreadable formats, ensuring that unauthorized parties cannot access it.

At Rest and In Transit: Encrypt data stored on servers, devices, and backups, as well as data transmitted over networks.

Key Management: Securely manage encryption keys using dedicated tools or hardware security modules (HSMs).

4. Protecting Data on Personal Devices

The use of personal devices in remote work necessitates additional safeguards:

Data Loss Prevention (DLP): Implement DLP solutions to monitor and control the flow of sensitive information.

Containerization: Use tools that create secure "containers" for work-related data, isolating it from personal files.

5. Ensuring Privacy in Communication

Organizations must respect employees' privacy while maintaining security:

Transparency: Clearly communicate how employee data is collected, used, and stored.

Privacy-by-Design: Integrate privacy considerations into the development and deployment of communication tools.

Anonymization and Pseudonymization: Apply techniques that protect personal data by removing or masking identifiers.

6. Compliance with Data Protection Regulations

Understanding and adhering to global and local data protection laws are non-negotiable:

GDPR: Focuses on protecting EU citizens' personal data and requires organizations to obtain explicit consent for data processing.

CCPA: Grants California residents rights to access, delete, and opt out of data collection.

ISO 27001: Provides an internationally recognized standard for information security management.

7. Auditing and Continuous Improvement

Data protection is not a one-time effort. Regular audits and assessments ensure ongoing compliance and effectiveness:

Internal Audits: Conduct periodic reviews of policies, tools, and practices to identify gaps.

Third-Party Assessments: Engage external experts to validate security measures and provide recommendations.

Continuous Training: Update employees on evolving threats and best practices to maintain vigilance.

By addressing cybersecurity and data protection comprehensively, organizations can ensure that their distributed teams communicate securely and efficiently. These measures not only protect sensitive information but also foster trust among employees, clients, and stakeholders.

10. Leveraging Advanced Technologies

The rapid evolution of technology has been pivotal in enabling remote and hybrid work models, and the role of advanced technologies is only expanding. Artificial intelligence (AI), automation, virtual reality (VR), and augmented reality (AR) have become central to improving efficiency, fostering collaboration, and redefining how distributed teams operate. This chapter explores how organizations can harness these cutting-edge tools to enhance the remote work experience and overcome challenges inherent in distributed setups.

Role of AI and Automation in Remote Work

Artificial intelligence and automation are transforming the remote work landscape by optimizing processes, improving decision-making, and reducing manual workloads. These technologies have redefined how organizations manage tasks, interact with employees, and deliver results. AI, with its ability to analyze large datasets and derive actionable insights, has become indispensable for streamlining operations. Automation, on the other hand, takes care of repetitive tasks, enabling employees to focus on higher-value activities. Together, they form a powerful duo for creating efficient remote workflows.

AI-powered tools are particularly valuable in areas like communication and project management. For instance, chatbots integrated into collaboration platforms handle routine queries, freeing up time for human interaction. AI algorithms can automatically schedule meetings by analyzing participants' availability, optimizing calendar management for distributed teams across time zones. These tools significantly reduce administrative overhead and ensure seamless coordination among team members, no matter where they are located. Similarly, AI-driven language translation tools facilitate real-time communication among diverse teams, breaking language barriers and fostering inclusivity in global operations.

In performance management, AI is instrumental in setting and tracking goals, providing personalized feedback, and identifying training needs. For instance, AI-based analytics tools monitor employee productivity by assessing engagement metrics such as task completion rates, response times, and overall output. These insights help managers make data-driven decisions to improve team performance while respecting individual work styles. Additionally, AI-powered platforms can predict employee burnout by analyzing work patterns, enabling proactive interventions to maintain well-being in remote environments.

Automation plays a crucial role in streamlining routine and repetitive tasks, especially in areas like HR, finance, and IT support. Automated workflows handle processes such as onboarding new employees, approving expense reports, and resolving common IT issues without human intervention. For example, Robotic Process Automation (RPA) is frequently employed to automate data entry, file management, and report generation. These technologies enhance productivity and reduce errors, which is particularly beneficial in remote work settings where traditional oversight mechanisms may be less effective.

AI also enhances cybersecurity in distributed work environments. Machine learning algorithms can detect anomalies in network traffic, identify phishing attempts, and respond to potential breaches in real time. These systems continuously adapt to emerging threats, providing a robust defense against the growing number of cyber risks faced by remote teams. In addition, AI-powered identity verification systems ensure secure access to sensitive information, further strengthening organizational defenses.

AI and automation are also key to improving customer interactions in remote setups. AI-powered customer service chatbots are available 24/7 to address inquiries, troubleshoot issues, and provide personalized recommendations. These tools enhance the customer experience while reducing the workload on human representatives. Similarly, automated email marketing campaigns and AI-driven social media management tools enable companies to maintain consistent and effective communication with their audience.

Virtual and Augmented Reality for Collaboration

Virtual reality (VR) and augmented reality (AR) are emerging as transformative tools for collaboration, offering immersive experiences that bridge the gap between physical and virtual workspaces. VR creates entirely virtual environments, while AR overlays digital information onto the real world. Both technologies have significant potential to enhance teamwork, creativity, and problem-solving in remote work settings.

One of the primary applications of VR in remote work is the creation of virtual meeting spaces. Unlike traditional video calls, VR meetings provide a sense of presence, allowing participants to interact in a shared environment as avatars. These environments can be customized to resemble traditional office spaces, creative studios, or even informal settings like cafes. This immersive experience fosters engagement, making virtual meetings feel more natural and productive. VR tools like Spatial and Engage are already enabling organizations to host brainstorming sessions, training workshops, and client presentations in virtual spaces.

AR, on the other hand, is particularly useful for collaboration in industries that require real-time problem-solving. For instance, AR technology enables remote technicians to provide on-site support by overlaying instructions and annotations onto live video feeds. This capability is invaluable in fields like manufacturing, healthcare, and engineering, where hands-on expertise is often required but not always available locally. AR platforms like Microsoft HoloLens and TeamViewer Pilot are revolutionizing how teams collaborate on complex tasks, regardless of geographical constraints.

Training and onboarding are other areas where VR and AR excel. Virtual reality simulations provide a safe and controlled environment for employees to learn new skills, practice complex procedures, and gain hands-on experience. For example, VR is used in healthcare to train surgeons, in aviation to simulate flight scenarios, and in customer service to practice handling challenging interactions. Similarly, AR can guide new hires through equipment setup, software usage, and company workflows by overlaying step-by-step instructions on their devices. These immersive training methods improve knowledge retention and confidence among employees, making them particularly effective for remote teams.

The use of VR and AR is also expanding in design and prototyping. Virtual reality enables designers and engineers to create and manipulate 3D models collaboratively, eliminating the need for physical prototypes. This approach accelerates the design process, reduces costs, and allows for more creative experimentation. AR complements this by enabling real-world visualization of designs, allowing stakeholders to interact with virtual models in physical spaces. These capabilities are particularly valuable in industries like architecture, automotive, and consumer goods, where innovation and precision are paramount.

Another promising application of AR is in remote sales and marketing. Sales teams can use augmented reality to demonstrate products to clients, offering an interactive and engaging experience that traditional methods cannot match. For instance, AR allows customers to visualize how furniture would look in their homes or how machinery would fit into their facilities. This level of personalization enhances the sales process and builds stronger connections with customers.

Despite their immense potential, VR and AR technologies face challenges such as high costs, technical limitations, and the need for specialized hardware. However, ongoing advancements are making these tools more accessible and affordable. For example, standalone VR headsets like the Oculus Quest eliminate the need for high-end computers, while AR applications can now run on standard smartphones and tablets. As these technologies continue to evolve, their integration into remote work setups is expected to grow exponentially.

In conclusion, AI, automation, VR, and AR are redefining how organizations approach remote work. These advanced technologies not only address the challenges of distributed teams but also unlock new opportunities for innovation, collaboration, and growth. By leveraging these tools effectively, organizations can create a more connected, productive, and secure remote work environment that meets the demands of the modern workforce. As these technologies continue to evolve, their role in shaping the future of work will become increasingly significant.

Part 4: Work-Life Balance in Remote Work

11. Challenges of Work-Life Balance in Distributed Work

Common Struggles: Overwork, Isolation, and Burnout

Remote and hybrid work models have created unparalleled flexibility for employees, but they also come with significant challenges in maintaining work-life balance. Among these challenges, overwork, isolation, and burnout are some of the most pressing issues faced by distributed teams. Understanding these struggles, their root causes, and potential solutions is essential for building sustainable work environments.

Overwork

One of the paradoxes of remote work is that while it eliminates commutes and provides more personal time in theory, it often leads to overwork in practice. Without the physical boundary of an office, employees frequently find it difficult to "switch off." This phenomenon, known as the "always-on culture," is driven by several factors.

First, the integration of work into home life often blurs the line between professional and personal time. Employees working from home may feel compelled to respond to emails or complete tasks outside regular hours, leading to extended workdays. Managers may unintentionally exacerbate this by scheduling meetings early in the morning or late at night to accommodate time zone differences in distributed teams. While these practices may seem necessary for global collaboration, they disrupt personal routines and contribute to fatigue.

Second, the lack of clear expectations around availability can lead employees to overcompensate. Many remote workers fear being perceived as less productive or engaged compared to their office-based counterparts. As a result, they work longer hours or take on additional responsibilities to prove their value. Over time, this can lead to a decline in productivity, creativity, and overall well-being.

Third, technology plays a role in perpetuating overwork. Instant messaging apps, video conferencing platforms, and project management tools have made communication seamless but also relentless. Notifications and alerts often interrupt personal time, creating a sense of urgency to respond even when it is not critical. This constant connectivity contributes to cognitive overload and makes it difficult for employees to disengage from work.

To address overwork, organizations must establish clear boundaries and expectations. For example, implementing "no-meeting days" or setting specific hours for team-wide communication can help employees manage their time more effectively. Encouraging managers to model healthy behaviors, such as avoiding emails after hours, can also foster a culture that prioritizes work-life balance. Moreover, providing resources like time management training or mindfulness programs can empower employees to maintain boundaries and focus on their well-being.

Isolation

Remote work has also brought the challenge of isolation to the forefront. Unlike traditional office settings, distributed teams lack opportunities for informal interactions, such as watercooler conversations or lunch breaks. These seemingly trivial moments play a significant role in building camaraderie and fostering a sense of belonging.

Isolation can manifest in different ways depending on the individual's circumstances. Employees who live alone may experience social isolation, feeling disconnected from colleagues and the outside world. Those with families may face emotional isolation if they lack support in navigating the complexities of remote work. Over time, isolation can lead to feelings of loneliness, reduced job satisfaction, and even depression.

Moreover, isolation disproportionately affects certain groups within distributed teams. For example, new hires or junior employees may find it particularly challenging to integrate into a team without the benefit of face-to-face interactions. Similarly, employees in remote locations with limited access to resources or social activities may feel left out of organizational culture and decision-making processes.

Organizations must adopt a proactive approach to combat isolation. Regular virtual check-ins, team-building activities, and informal gatherings can help employees feel connected and valued. For example, hosting virtual coffee chats or trivia nights allows colleagues to interact in a non-work context. In addition, mentorship programs can provide guidance and support for employees who feel isolated, fostering a sense of inclusion.

Technology can also play a role in mitigating isolation. Collaboration tools like Slack or Microsoft Teams enable employees to communicate informally, share interests, and celebrate achievements. Similarly, virtual reality platforms can recreate the experience of being in a shared physical space, enhancing the sense of presence and connection. However, organizations must balance these efforts with the need to avoid overloading employees with digital interactions.

Burnout

Burnout is perhaps the most severe consequence of prolonged overwork and isolation. Characterized by emotional exhaustion, cynicism, and reduced performance, burnout is a growing concern in distributed work environments. The lack of physical separation between work and home life, combined with the pressures of remote collaboration, makes employees particularly vulnerable to this condition.

One of the key drivers of burnout in remote settings is the absence of regular breaks and downtime. Without the structure of an office routine, employees may skip lunch or work through weekends, leaving little time for recovery. Additionally, the monotony of working in the same environment every day can erode motivation and creativity, further contributing to burnout.

Another factor is the psychological toll of navigating constant uncertainty. Remote workers often face challenges such as unstable internet connections, lack of access to necessary tools, or unclear instructions from managers. These issues create additional stress and frustration, which can accumulate over time.

Burnout is also influenced by organizational culture. In environments that prioritize productivity over well-being, employees may feel pressured to overperform at the expense of their health. For example, unrealistic deadlines or excessive workloads can lead to chronic stress, making it difficult for employees to maintain a healthy work-life balance.

To address burnout, organizations must focus on prevention and support. This begins with recognizing the signs of burnout, such as decreased engagement, irritability, or frequent absenteeism. Managers should create an open environment where employees feel comfortable discussing their challenges and seeking help. Providing access to mental health resources, such as counseling or wellness programs, can also help employees cope with stress.

Flexibility is another critical factor in preventing burnout. Allowing employees to set their schedules, take mental health days, or choose their preferred working hours can reduce stress and improve work-life balance. Additionally, fostering a culture that values quality over quantity ensures that employees feel supported rather than overwhelmed.

Differences in Cultural Perceptions of Work-Life Boundaries

Work-life balance is not a one-size-fits-all concept; cultural differences significantly influence how employees perceive and manage boundaries between work and personal life. These differences can create challenges for distributed teams operating across regions with varying norms and expectations.

In some cultures, such as the United States and Northern Europe, work-life balance is viewed as a personal responsibility. Employees are encouraged to set boundaries and prioritize their well-being, and organizations often provide flexible work arrangements to support this. For example, companies in Scandinavia are known for their generous parental leave policies and emphasis on reducing working hours to promote life satisfaction.

In contrast, cultures in East Asia, such as Japan and South Korea, often emphasize dedication and loyalty to the workplace. Long working hours and a strong focus on achieving organizational goals are deeply ingrained in these societies. Employees in such cultures may feel reluctant to take breaks or set boundaries, viewing it as a sign of commitment. This can lead to challenges when integrating remote work practices that rely on individual autonomy.

Similarly, countries with collectivist cultures, such as India and Brazil, often prioritize family and community over individual needs. In these contexts, work-life balance is closely tied to the well-being of the family unit. Remote work may blur the lines between professional and personal responsibilities, leading to unique challenges in managing both effectively.

Organizations operating in diverse cultural environments must navigate these differences with sensitivity and adaptability.

Providing training on cross-cultural communication can help teams understand and respect varying perspectives on work-life balance. Managers should also tailor their approaches to meet the needs of their employees, taking into account cultural norms and preferences.

Ultimately, achieving work-life balance in distributed work settings requires a combination of individual effort and organizational support. By addressing common struggles like overwork, isolation, and burnout, and recognizing cultural differences, organizations can create an environment where employees thrive both personally and professionally. This not only enhances employee satisfaction but also contributes to long-term success in the ever-evolving world of remote work.

12. Promoting Employee Well-being

Mental Health Resources and Initiatives

The shift to remote and hybrid work has brought mental health to the forefront of workplace priorities. While these models offer greater flexibility, they also present challenges that can strain employees' emotional and psychological well-being. From isolation and overwork to navigating uncertainties, distributed teams face stressors that demand proactive measures to promote mental health. Organizations that prioritize mental health resources and initiatives can foster a culture of resilience, trust, and productivity.

One of the most effective ways to support mental health is by providing access to professional resources. Many companies now offer Employee Assistance Programs (EAPs) that include confidential counseling services, stress management workshops, and access to mental health professionals. These programs help employees navigate personal and professional challenges, ensuring they feel supported even when working remotely. For example, a virtual EAP platform can allow employees to schedule counseling sessions at their convenience, eliminating barriers to seeking help.

Organizations can also implement mindfulness and wellness programs tailored to the unique challenges of remote work. Guided meditation sessions, yoga classes, and resilience training are examples of initiatives that help employees manage stress and improve focus. Technology can further enhance these efforts; apps like Headspace or Calm, when offered as part of a corporate wellness package, make mental health resources accessible to employees across time zones.

Training managers to recognize signs of mental health struggles is another critical aspect. Leaders in distributed teams may not have the same visibility into employees' emotional states as they would in a traditional office setting. Equipping them with tools to identify burnout, disengagement, or stress enables timely intervention. Regular one-on-one check-ins that include conversations about well-being, rather than solely focusing on tasks, can foster open communication and a supportive atmosphere.

Promoting a stigma-free environment around mental health is essential for these initiatives to succeed. Employees must feel comfortable discussing their struggles without fear of judgment or repercussions. Organizations can normalize these conversations by sharing stories of leaders or colleagues who have sought support and thrived. Additionally, establishing dedicated mental health days or allowing employees to take leave without specifying reasons shows a commitment to their overall well-being.

Global organizations should also consider cultural nuances in mental health initiatives. In some regions, discussing mental health remains taboo, requiring a more discreet and culturally sensitive approach. Offering diverse resources, such as multilingual counseling services or region-specific wellness programs, ensures inclusivity. Tailoring programs to different cultural contexts demonstrates a genuine commitment to employee well-being and enhances participation.

Encouraging Breaks and Maintaining Work Boundaries

While flexibility is a hallmark of remote work, it often leads to the unintended consequence of blurred boundaries between professional and personal life. Many employees struggle to disconnect, leading to overwork, fatigue, and diminished productivity. Encouraging breaks and maintaining work boundaries are essential strategies to promote long-term well-being.

Breaks are more than just a pause from work; they are vital for mental clarity, creativity, and sustained performance. Research shows that short breaks throughout the day can significantly enhance focus and reduce stress. However, remote employees often skip breaks due to a lack of natural cues, such as colleagues leaving for lunch or coffee. Organizations can counteract this by integrating structured breaks into the workday. For example, introducing a "10-minute mindfulness break" during team meetings or encouraging employees to step away from their screens every hour helps build healthy habits.

Another effective approach is gamifying break time. Companies can use digital platforms to create challenges, such as completing a 15-minute walk or preparing a healthy snack. These initiatives foster engagement while encouraging employees to prioritize self-care. Additionally, virtual coworking sessions, where employees work alongside each other with scheduled breaks, can mimic the rhythm of an office environment and reinforce the importance of downtime.

Maintaining boundaries in remote work requires both individual effort and organizational support. Employees need tools and strategies to separate work from personal life effectively. Providing training on time management and boundary-setting can empower employees to create routines that promote balance. For example, using a dedicated workspace, setting specific work hours, and disabling notifications outside these hours can help employees delineate their professional and personal spheres.

Organizations play a crucial role in reinforcing these boundaries. Leaders should model healthy behaviors, such as logging off at reasonable hours and refraining from sending late-night emails. Policies that discourage after-hours communication or require employees to use their vacation days can further reinforce a culture of balance. For instance, some companies implement "no-email weekends" or enforce mandatory time off to ensure employees recharge.

Technology can also support boundary maintenance. Features like "Do Not Disturb" modes on collaboration platforms or automatic status updates indicating off-hours can help employees avoid interruptions. Additionally, organizations can invest in tools that monitor work hours and send reminders to take breaks or end the workday. These systems demonstrate a commitment to employee well-being while mitigating the risks of overwork.

Promoting boundaries also involves recognizing the unique challenges faced by different employee groups. For example, working parents may need flexible schedules to accommodate caregiving responsibilities, while employees in different time zones may struggle with overlapping work hours. Tailoring support to individual needs ensures inclusivity and helps all team members achieve balance.

In conclusion, promoting employee well-being in remote and hybrid work environments requires a comprehensive approach that addresses mental health and work-life balance. Providing accessible resources, encouraging breaks, and fostering clear boundaries not only enhances employee satisfaction but also drives organizational success. By prioritizing well-being, companies can create resilient and engaged teams equipped to navigate the complexities of distributed work.

13. Creating Flexible Policies for Work-Life Balance

Crafting Policies That Support Both Employees and Organizations

In the evolving landscape of remote and hybrid work, crafting flexible policies that balance organizational goals with employee well-being is a cornerstone for long-term success. Such policies not only enhance productivity but also foster loyalty, reduce turnover, and establish a supportive workplace culture. Developing these policies requires a nuanced approach that considers the diverse needs of employees while aligning with the organization's strategic objectives.

One key area is the flexibility in working hours. Traditional 9-to-5 schedules often clash with the varied personal responsibilities of remote employees. Offering flexible work schedules, such as staggered start and end times or compressed workweeks, can empower employees to manage their professional and personal lives effectively. For example, an employee with caregiving duties may prefer to start earlier and finish in the afternoon, while another may be more productive during unconventional hours. Such flexibility not only enhances work-life balance but also leads to higher job satisfaction and productivity.

Another effective policy is implementing location flexibility. Allowing employees to work from different locations, whether from home, a co-working space, or even another country, enables them to optimize their work environment. This approach is particularly valuable for employees who may need to relocate temporarily or prefer a change of scenery to maintain motivation. Organizations can formalize this flexibility by introducing "work from anywhere" policies, provided that cybersecurity and compliance measures are in place.

Time-off policies are also critical in fostering balance. Encouraging employees to take regular breaks and vacations helps prevent burnout and rejuvenates their energy levels. Companies can adopt unlimited or flexible paid time-off policies, as seen in organizations like Netflix, which prioritize results over hours worked. However, the success of such policies relies on creating a culture where taking time off is normalized and encouraged, rather than perceived as a lack of commitment.

Additionally, offering policies that address specific employee needs can significantly enhance balance. Parental leave, caregiver support programs, and mental health days are examples of tailored policies that reflect an organization's commitment to holistic well-being. For instance, extended parental leave policies not only support new parents but also promote gender equality by enabling both mothers and fathers to take time off without career repercussions.

Transparent communication is essential to the success of these policies. Employees must clearly understand what is available to them and how to access these benefits. Organizations can use digital tools and platforms to communicate policies effectively, such as creating an online portal with detailed guidelines and FAQs. Providing regular training sessions for managers ensures that they understand these policies and can guide their teams in utilizing them.

Role of HR in Ensuring Well-Being

Human Resources (HR) plays a pivotal role in shaping, implementing, and monitoring policies that promote work-life balance in remote and hybrid settings. As the bridge between leadership and employees, HR must balance organizational objectives with employee welfare, ensuring that policies are practical, inclusive, and adaptable.

One of HR's primary responsibilities is conducting needs assessments to understand the unique challenges faced by employees in distributed work models. Surveys, focus groups, and feedback sessions are invaluable tools for gathering insights into employees' preferences, struggles, and expectations. For example, HR can identify if employees require more support in managing workload, better access to mental health resources, or improvements in communication technologies. These findings inform the development of targeted policies that address actual needs rather than assumptions.

HR also plays a critical role in promoting equity and inclusion in policy design. Remote and hybrid workforces are often diverse, with employees operating across different geographies, cultures, and socio-economic backgrounds. Policies must reflect this diversity to ensure fairness. For instance, offering a flexible work-from-home stipend acknowledges that not all employees have access to a dedicated workspace or high-speed internet. Similarly, providing resources in multiple languages or tailoring policies to accommodate local labor laws demonstrates an inclusive approach.

Ensuring employee well-being extends beyond policy creation to its effective implementation. HR teams must train managers to lead with empathy and adaptability, particularly in remote settings where physical cues are absent. Leaders should be equipped to recognize signs of stress or disengagement and respond proactively. For example, if an employee consistently works late hours despite flexible scheduling, HR can intervene to understand the root cause and provide support.

HR also acts as the custodian of mental health initiatives within the organization. By partnering with external providers, HR can offer access to counseling, workshops, and wellness programs tailored to the demands of remote work. These programs can be supplemented with internal campaigns that encourage employees to prioritize their well-being, such as promoting mental health awareness months or organizing virtual fitness challenges.

Technology is another area where HR can make a significant impact. Digital tools enable HR to monitor policy effectiveness, gather feedback, and make data-driven adjustments. For instance, analytics platforms can track employee engagement, usage of wellness resources, and adherence to work-life balance guidelines. This data helps HR identify trends and address gaps proactively.

Continuous improvement is key to ensuring that policies remain relevant and effective. Regularly reviewing policies in response to employee feedback and organizational changes helps maintain alignment. For example, as new technologies emerge or workforce demographics shift, HR can update policies to reflect these changes. Involving employees in the review process fosters a sense of ownership and trust, making them more likely to embrace and advocate for these policies.

In conclusion, creating flexible policies for work-life balance requires a collaborative effort between leadership, HR, and employees. By prioritizing flexibility, inclusivity, and continuous improvement, organizations can build a supportive environment where employees thrive. HR's role as a strategic partner ensures that these policies not only enhance individual well-being but also contribute to the organization's long-term success in navigating the complexities of remote and hybrid work.

Part 5: Case Studies and Best Practices

14. Success Stories in Remote and Hybrid Work

Examples from Leading Companies

Remote and hybrid work models have transformed the way organizations operate, enabling flexibility and resilience. Many leading companies have successfully implemented these models, setting benchmarks for the industry. Their strategies offer valuable insights into what works and how challenges can be overcome.

Microsoft

As a global technology giant, Microsoft adopted a hybrid work strategy that emphasizes flexibility and inclusivity. Recognizing the varied needs of its workforce, the company introduced a policy allowing employees to work remotely up to 50% of the time without manager approval. This flexibility enables employees to balance work and personal responsibilities. Microsoft also invested heavily in enhancing its collaboration tools, such as Microsoft Teams, to support seamless communication and teamwork.

The company's emphasis on employee well-being is another pillar of its success. Microsoft offers mindfulness resources, stress management workshops, and mental health support, ensuring employees are equipped to thrive in remote and hybrid settings. By prioritizing communication, the company conducted regular "pulse surveys" to gauge employee sentiment, using the feedback to refine its policies.

Lessons Learned:

Flexibility drives employee satisfaction and productivity.

Continuous feedback loops are essential for fine-tuning remote work strategies.

Investing in technology facilitates effective collaboration.

GitLab

GitLab operates as an all-remote company, with employees spread across more than 65 countries. The company's success lies in its transparency and documentation. GitLab maintains an extensive handbook that outlines every aspect of its operations, from communication protocols to decision-making processes. This resource ensures that all employees, regardless of location, have access to the same information, reducing ambiguity and fostering alignment.

The company also emphasizes asynchronous communication to accommodate diverse time zones. By documenting meetings and discussions, GitLab minimizes the need for real-time interactions, enabling employees to work at their own pace. Furthermore, GitLab prioritizes team bonding through virtual coffee chats and global meetups, fostering a sense of community despite geographical distances.

Lessons Learned:

Comprehensive documentation eliminates confusion and promotes consistency.

Asynchronous communication enhances inclusivity and efficiency.

Intentional team-building activities strengthen connections in distributed teams.

Spotify

Spotify implemented its "Work from Anywhere" policy, empowering employees to choose where they work—be it at home, in the office, or a combination of both. The policy reflects Spotify's trust in its employees and its commitment to diversity. The company also reimagined its office spaces to serve as collaboration hubs rather than traditional workplaces. This shift enables employees to come together for brainstorming sessions, team events, or when they need a change of scenery.

Spotify provides a stipend for home office setups, ensuring employees have the tools they need to succeed. Additionally, the company supports work-life balance through generous parental leave policies, mental health days, and flexible working hours. By focusing on autonomy and support, Spotify has cultivated a culture of trust and innovation.

Lessons Learned:

Empowering employees to choose their work environment boosts engagement.

Redesigning office spaces for collaboration aligns with hybrid work needs.

Providing resources and support ensures employees are equipped for success.

Lessons Learned from Successful Implementations

The experiences of these leading companies highlight several key principles that contribute to successful remote and hybrid work models:

Flexibility is Key: Allowing employees to tailor their work arrangements enhances productivity and job satisfaction. Policies should accommodate different preferences, such as remote, hybrid, or office-based work.

Leverage Technology: Robust collaboration tools are essential for seamless communication and teamwork. Organizations should invest in platforms that support both synchronous and asynchronous communication, ensuring inclusivity across time zones.

Prioritize Employee Well-Being: Offering mental health resources, flexible schedules, and support systems fosters resilience and engagement. Employees who feel cared for are more likely to stay motivated and loyal.

Foster a Sense of Community: Building connections in distributed teams requires intentional efforts. Virtual team-building activities, regular check-ins, and occasional in-person gatherings can strengthen bonds and reinforce company culture.

Encourage Feedback and Adaptability: Regularly seeking employee input through surveys or forums helps organizations identify areas for improvement. Being open to change ensures policies remain relevant and effective.

Focus on Inclusivity: Remote and hybrid work models should cater to diverse needs. Providing resources for different time zones, cultural backgrounds, and work styles ensures that all employees feel valued and supported.

Document Everything: Clear and accessible documentation of policies, processes, and expectations reduces confusion and enhances transparency. This is especially important in distributed teams where face-to-face interactions are limited.

Redefine Success Metrics: Traditional performance metrics may not align with remote work. Organizations should focus on outcomes and results rather than hours worked or physical presence.

By studying these success stories and implementing their lessons, organizations can navigate the complexities of remote and hybrid work while fostering a culture of flexibility, trust, and innovation.

15. Overcoming Common Challenges

Strategies to Address Team Disconnect, Tech Failures, and Resistance to Change

Remote and hybrid work models, while offering flexibility and a range of benefits, also introduce a unique set of challenges that organizations must navigate to ensure long-term success. Among these challenges, team disconnect, technological failures, and resistance to change are among the most prevalent. Addressing these challenges proactively requires a combination of strategic planning, effective communication, and a willingness to adapt to the changing dynamics of the workplace. In this chapter, we will explore strategies for overcoming these obstacles and ensuring that teams remain connected, productive, and resilient.

Addressing Team Disconnect

1. Fostering Clear and Consistent Communication

Team disconnect often arises when employees feel isolated or out of the loop, particularly in remote and hybrid work settings. The absence of spontaneous interactions that typically occur in a traditional office environment can lead to misunderstandings, misaligned priorities, and reduced collaboration. To combat this, clear and consistent communication must be prioritized.

One effective strategy is the implementation of regular team check-ins, both at the individual and team levels. These can take the form of daily or weekly stand-ups, where employees discuss their goals, challenges, and progress. Virtual team meetings should be structured to ensure every participant has the opportunity to speak, and updates are shared clearly. This creates a routine that reinforces connection and accountability.

Additionally, companies should leverage a range of communication channels to suit different preferences and contexts. Email, instant messaging platforms (such as Slack), video conferencing tools (like Zoom), and project management software (such as Asana or Trello) should be used strategically to ensure seamless communication across different time zones and geographical locations. Utilizing asynchronous communication, where possible, can also address the challenges of varying work hours and time zones.

2. Building a Strong Team Culture

Team culture is critical in maintaining connection among remote employees. While it can be challenging to foster a sense of camaraderie in a virtual environment, it is possible with intentional effort. Teams can engage in regular virtual social activities, such as happy hours, virtual coffee breaks, or team-building games. These activities, although informal, can help break down barriers, encourage bonding, and create a sense of belonging.

Moreover, leaders should make an effort to regularly recognize and celebrate achievements. Public praise, whether in virtual meetings or on internal communication platforms, can reinforce a positive team atmosphere and highlight the value of individual contributions. Creating spaces where employees feel safe to share both personal and professional milestones fosters an environment of openness and mutual support.

3. Establishing Clear Roles and Expectations

When teams are working remotely, there is often a lack of visibility into each other's daily activities, which can contribute to feelings of disconnect. To mitigate this, it is essential to establish clear roles and expectations from the outset. Detailed project plans, well-defined responsibilities, and transparent timelines help employees understand their role within the broader team and prevent overlaps or misunderstandings. This clarity can enhance both productivity and cohesion.

Managing Tech Failures

1. Investing in Reliable Technology

One of the most significant challenges in remote and hybrid work is the risk of technology failures. From poor internet connections to malfunctioning software or outdated hardware, technical issues can disrupt workflows and lead to frustration. To mitigate these risks, companies must invest in reliable, high-performance technology.

This includes providing employees with up-to-date hardware, such as laptops with sufficient processing power and high-quality webcams, as well as ensuring access to robust software solutions that are compatible with team needs. Cloud-based collaboration tools, which allow for seamless document sharing and real-time collaboration, are essential for supporting hybrid work models. Popular tools like Google Workspace or Microsoft Office 365 should be used to streamline collaboration and reduce the chance of technological hiccups.

In addition, organizations should work with their IT teams to set up contingency plans for dealing with technical issues. This includes ensuring that employees have access to technical support, whether through a helpdesk, a troubleshooting guide, or live assistance. Regular maintenance and software updates are critical to avoiding system outages and keeping tools running smoothly.

2. Training Employees on Tools and Technology

Even with the best tools in place, technology can still be a source of frustration if employees are not properly trained on how to use them effectively. Offering regular training sessions on new tools, software updates, and best practices for troubleshooting can reduce confusion and minimize downtime.

Moreover, creating user-friendly resources, such as tutorial videos, FAQs, or knowledge bases, allows employees to quickly solve minor tech issues on their own. This empowers employees to work more independently and efficiently, while reducing reliance on IT support for basic technical challenges.

3. Implementing Redundancy Systems

To prevent major disruptions in case of tech failures, organizations should have backup systems and redundancies in place. This could include cloud backups for important data, redundant communication channels (such as backup email services), and alternative platforms for video conferencing (in case a primary platform experiences issues). Having these systems in place ensures that employees can continue working smoothly, even if one tool or system fails.

Overcoming Resistance to Change

1. Transparent Communication About Change

Resistance to change is a natural response in many work environments, especially when employees are asked to adapt to new processes, tools, or work models. In the context of remote and hybrid work, employees may be hesitant to embrace new policies, technologies, or ways of collaborating. The key to overcoming resistance is transparent and consistent communication.

Before implementing any changes, organizations should clearly explain the reasons behind them, the expected benefits, and how they will impact employees. Engaging employees early in the process and soliciting their feedback can also help them feel more involved in the decision-making process. This approach fosters trust and makes employees feel like active participants in the transformation, rather than passive recipients of change.

2. Training and Support for Adaptation

Resistance often stems from a lack of understanding or fear of the unknown. To combat this, organizations should provide comprehensive training and resources to support employees through the transition. Whether it's learning new software, adjusting to a hybrid work environment, or shifting to a results-oriented approach, training sessions, webinars, and one-on-one coaching can help employees feel more confident and capable.

Additionally, assigning "change champions" within the organization—employees who are particularly enthusiastic about the change—can provide peer support and guidance. These change champions can answer questions, offer assistance, and share their experiences, helping to normalize the transition.

3. Gradual Implementation and Flexibility

Implementing change gradually rather than all at once allows employees to adjust at their own pace. This approach reduces the feeling of being overwhelmed and allows leaders to monitor progress, gather feedback, and make necessary adjustments. Additionally, offering flexibility during the transition period, such as temporary hybrid models or extended timeframes for adopting new tools, can help ease the adjustment process.

Finally, recognizing and celebrating small wins throughout the transition period can build momentum and reduce resistance. When employees see that the changes are yielding positive results—such as increased productivity or better work-life balance—they are more likely to embrace the shift wholeheartedly.

The challenges of team disconnect, technology failures, and resistance to change are inherent in remote and hybrid work models, but they are not insurmountable. By implementing clear communication strategies, investing in reliable technology, and fostering a culture of transparency and adaptability, organizations can overcome these challenges. Proactively addressing these obstacles ensures that teams remain connected, productive, and resilient, ultimately creating a positive and thriving work environment for remote and hybrid employees.

16. Customizing Models for Your Organization

Tailoring Work Models Based on Company Size, Culture, and Industry

The rise of remote and hybrid work models has proven that flexibility is key to fostering productivity, improving employee well-being, and ensuring operational efficiency. However, while a one-size-fits-all approach to these work models may sound appealing, it's critical for organizations to tailor their strategies based on their unique characteristics—whether that be company size, culture, or industry. Customizing a work model that aligns with these factors is vital for achieving long-term success and engagement. This chapter explores how organizations can personalize their remote or hybrid work models to suit their specific needs, providing actionable strategies for adapting to size, culture, and industry considerations.

Tailoring Work Models Based on Company Size

1. Small Organizations: Personalized, Flexible Work Models

In smaller organizations, the benefit of a more personalized, flexible approach to remote and hybrid work is particularly pronounced. With fewer layers of management, there's often more agility in decision-making, allowing for quicker implementation of work models that can be easily adjusted based on the evolving needs of employees and business goals.

For smaller companies, a hybrid model where employees work from the office for certain collaborative activities (e.g., brainstorming sessions or team-building events) and work remotely the rest of the time can work well. The flexibility in remote work allows for efficient time management and supports work-life balance, while in-office interactions help maintain the close-knit, collaborative culture that is often a hallmark of smaller organizations.

Small organizations can also leverage this flexibility to tailor their remote work models to individual employee preferences. For example, employees in a smaller organization may be offered the option to fully work remotely, or they may have a hybrid arrangement that allows for some office presence when required, but the schedules are often more fluid. This high level of customization helps foster employee loyalty, as they feel empowered by the autonomy and trust granted to them.

However, the challenge in smaller organizations often lies in maintaining communication and collaboration. The key here is setting clear expectations, using digital tools effectively, and ensuring that remote employees feel as included and valued as those working in the office. Regular virtual team meetings, one-on-ones, and social events can support a cohesive team environment.

2. Medium-Sized Organizations: Structuring for Efficiency and Scalability

As an organization grows in size, the hybrid or remote work model needs to be structured with more standardized systems and procedures. For medium-sized organizations, it is important to balance flexibility with consistency to ensure that all employees are working toward the same goals, regardless of location.

The remote and hybrid work model may need to be adjusted based on departments or job functions. For instance, creative teams might thrive with more in-person collaboration, while other departments—such as IT or customer service—may be more suited to remote work. Medium-sized companies may adopt a "hybrid with flexibility" model, where teams have the autonomy to choose the best work environment for their tasks but still adhere to core company-wide expectations for attendance and communication.

It's also essential to have clear systems in place for managing remote workers and ensuring accountability. This could involve using project management platforms (such as Asana, Monday.com, or Jira) to track tasks, setting regular check-ins, and implementing key performance indicators (KPIs) that focus on outcomes, not just time spent working. By establishing efficient structures and tools, medium-sized companies can ensure that remote employees remain productive, engaged, and aligned with the broader goals of the organization.

3. Large Organizations: Standardized Processes with Regional Flexibility

In large organizations, work models must be scalable and standardized to support thousands of employees across multiple teams, departments, or even regions. While standardization is crucial for consistency, regional and cultural differences often require a level of flexibility to accommodate different needs.

Large companies may need to offer flexible hybrid work models that provide varying degrees of remote work depending on the region or office location. For example, teams in one country or region may prefer a more traditional in-office model, while others may have adopted more remote-friendly environments. To ensure uniformity across these different regions, organizations can create a set of guidelines for remote work—such as core working hours, communication protocols, and performance expectations—that can be adjusted as needed.

At the same time, large organizations benefit from the use of enterprise-grade tools that help manage remote work at scale. These tools could include global communication platforms (e.g., Slack or Microsoft Teams), employee engagement tools, and project management systems that integrate with broader company operations. Additionally, larger organizations often have more resources available for training, technical support, and IT infrastructure, which can help mitigate some of the challenges associated with managing remote teams.

Tailoring Work Models Based on Company Culture

1. Collaborative Cultures: In-Person Collaboration and Flexibility

Organizations with a collaborative or creative culture tend to prioritize in-person interactions to foster brainstorming, idea-sharing, and team-building. For these types of companies, a hybrid work model that emphasizes in-office time for meetings, collaborative work, and social interaction is often the most effective.

Companies with collaborative cultures may designate specific days for teams to meet in person, ensuring that employees can come together for high-impact projects, group discussions, and networking opportunities. However, remote work can still play a key role in allowing employees to focus on independent tasks, manage their time effectively, and avoid distractions often found in the office environment.

That being said, even in a collaborative culture, it's essential to invest in technology that supports virtual teamwork. Video conferencing tools (Zoom, Google Meet), collaborative document editing platforms (Google Docs, Microsoft OneNote), and shared project management tools (Trello, Basecamp) allow teams to maintain continuous communication and collaboration, even when working remotely.

2. Autonomous Cultures: Trust-Based Hybrid Work

Organizations that value autonomy and individual responsibility may find that remote work is more aligned with their culture. These organizations tend to hire employees who are self-motivated and capable of working independently, and they thrive in environments where employees are given the freedom to manage their own schedules and deliverables. For these companies, the hybrid model should lean more heavily toward remote work with occasional in-office collaboration.

In autonomous cultures, the emphasis is placed on results rather than physical presence in the office. Trust is the cornerstone of these organizations, and as such, leaders must prioritize establishing clear performance metrics, open lines of communication, and flexible work arrangements that accommodate personal preferences and schedules.

To make the hybrid model work effectively in an autonomous culture, it's critical for organizations to focus on outcomes, not processes. This means defining clear goals, providing employees with the tools they need to succeed remotely, and offering regular check-ins without micromanaging. By fostering a culture of accountability and trust, these organizations can benefit from the flexibility of remote work without sacrificing performance or collaboration.

Tailoring Work Models Based on Industry

1. Tech and Knowledge-Based Industries: Flexibility for Innovation

In industries such as technology, software development, consulting, and other knowledge-based fields, remote and hybrid work models are often the easiest to implement. Many employees in these industries rely on computers and digital tools, which makes it possible for them to work effectively from any location. For these industries, adopting a hybrid or fully remote model can be highly advantageous in attracting top talent, reducing overhead costs, and enhancing productivity.

In tech-focused companies, it's not uncommon for employees to work entirely remotely, as long as they have the tools and systems needed to complete their tasks efficiently. To accommodate this, organizations should ensure that employees have access to cloud-based tools for file sharing, collaboration, and communication. Additionally, flexible hours may be essential for these employees, particularly when they are working with global teams across multiple time zones.

2. Customer Service and Healthcare: Balancing Remote and In-Office Work

Industries that require a high level of customer interaction—such as customer service, retail, and healthcare—may find that hybrid models work best. While certain roles within these industries can be handled remotely (such as customer service representatives who manage inquiries via email or phone), others require employees to be present in person to interact with customers directly. For these industries, work models need to balance the need for in-person interaction with the flexibility that remote work provides.

For instance, customer service representatives may work remotely for a portion of the week, but when dealing with complex issues or escalations, they may need to be in the office. Similarly, healthcare providers, such as medical professionals or therapists, may use telehealth technologies to meet with patients remotely but need to be on-site for physical exams or procedures.

3. Manufacturing and Logistics: Office Support for On-Site Operations

In industries such as manufacturing, logistics, and construction, where a significant portion of the work is done on-site, remote work may not be feasible for most roles.

However, certain administrative or back-office roles, such as HR, accounting, or IT support, can be executed remotely. In these cases, a hybrid model that allows administrative staff to work remotely while on-site workers perform physical tasks may be ideal.

Organizations in these industries can implement remote work for roles that don't directly affect the production line or customer-facing operations, while ensuring that workers on the ground have the necessary resources, tools, and support for their tasks. Balancing the practicalities of on-site work with the flexibility of remote work can improve efficiency, reduce costs, and help attract and retain talent in non-technical roles.

Customizing remote and hybrid work models based on company size, culture, and industry is essential for optimizing productivity, maintaining employee satisfaction, and fostering long-term success. Whether a company is small and nimble or large and complex, the ability to adapt work models to fit the needs of the organization and its employees will ensure that the transition to remote or hybrid work is effective, sustainable, and beneficial for all stakeholders involved. By taking the time to understand and implement tailored strategies, organizations can navigate the challenges of modern work environments and position themselves for success

Part 6: The Road Ahead

17. Continuous Improvement in Remote and Hybrid Work

Feedback Mechanisms and Iteration

The success of any organizational model, especially remote and hybrid work, hinges on its ability to evolve continuously. A static approach, where a company sets its processes once and assumes they will work indefinitely, is bound to fail as work dynamics shift. Feedback mechanisms and iteration are the core principles that drive continuous improvement in remote and hybrid work models. As remote work becomes a permanent feature of the business landscape, organizations must remain agile, regularly assessing what works, what doesn't, and where improvements can be made.

Feedback Mechanisms for Remote and Hybrid Work

The first and most important step toward continuous improvement is establishing reliable and comprehensive feedback channels. These channels ensure that employees at all levels have the opportunity to voice their experiences, challenges, and suggestions for improvement. The feedback loop not only fosters a sense of inclusion and empowerment but also helps organizations remain responsive to employee needs, optimizing productivity and morale.

1. Regular Employee Surveys

Surveys are one of the most effective tools for gauging employee sentiment in a remote or hybrid setting. These surveys can be used to collect data on various aspects of the work experience, including job satisfaction, communication effectiveness, team dynamics, and technology usage. Conducting surveys regularly—whether quarterly, biannually, or annually—allows the organization to stay attuned to employee needs and identify emerging trends.

To make surveys effective, they should cover both quantitative and qualitative data. Quantitative questions (using Likert scales or multiple-choice answers) can measure aspects like the effectiveness of remote work tools, while qualitative open-ended questions can provide insights into personal experiences and areas for improvement. The feedback collected should be acted upon quickly to demonstrate that employees' voices matter and to drive tangible changes in the work model.

2. One-on-One Meetings and Check-ins

In remote and hybrid environments, employees can often feel disconnected or isolated, especially if they work in different time zones or have limited direct contact with their managers. To address this, regular one-on-one meetings and check-ins are crucial. These personal meetings give employees the space to discuss their challenges, ask for support, and provide feedback on how the work environment is functioning.

Managers can use these sessions to gauge an employee's comfort with their hybrid or remote work arrangement, ask about any barriers to productivity, and explore potential solutions. One-on-one meetings can also serve as a chance for employees to suggest improvements, such as changes in communication methods, work schedules, or team processes.

3. Peer Feedback and Team Feedback Sessions

Another powerful tool for feedback is peer reviews or team feedback sessions. These meetings allow employees to share feedback with one another, which can help identify pain points that might otherwise go unnoticed by management. Team feedback sessions can focus on collaboration, communication, project timelines, and specific challenges related to remote or hybrid work. Such sessions encourage collective problem-solving, where teams work together to find solutions that improve the overall work model.

Team feedback can be structured formally or informally. Structured feedback sessions may include a roundtable format where every team member shares their thoughts on specific questions, while informal feedback can take place during regular team meetings, project debriefs, or even virtual coffee chats.

4. Employee Engagement Metrics

In hybrid and remote environments, traditional engagement metrics like office attendance are not useful for measuring the level of employee engagement. Instead, companies must rely on more sophisticated measures of engagement. These could include tracking the frequency of communication between employees, their participation in virtual meetings, contributions to collaborative projects, and other indicators of involvement.

Tools like Slack, Microsoft Teams, or other communication platforms can be used to analyze employee engagement in real-time. Some tools can track how often employees interact with team members, participate in group discussions, or attend virtual events. Regular analysis of these metrics helps organizations spot trends and take action if employees become disengaged or isolated.

Iteration: Adapting Based on Feedback

Once feedback has been gathered, the next critical step is iteration—actively applying the insights to continuously improve the work model. Iteration involves testing new approaches, measuring their impact, and refining them based on the results. By embedding an iterative mindset into the organizational culture, companies can make incremental changes that add up to significant improvements over time.

1. Identifying Key Areas for Change

Based on the feedback gathered through surveys, one-on-ones, and team meetings, the next step is identifying which aspects of the remote or hybrid work model require attention. Common areas for improvement might include communication tools, collaboration practices, work scheduling, or performance management techniques. Once these areas are identified, companies can prioritize which issues need to be addressed first.

For instance, if employees express frustration over inefficient virtual meetings, companies might invest in better conferencing technology or introduce guidelines for more focused and productive meetings. Similarly, if feedback shows that employees struggle with managing work-life boundaries, companies might consider implementing more structured hours, offering mental health support, or creating additional wellness programs.

2. Experimentation and Pilot Programs

When implementing changes based on feedback, it's important to adopt a test-and-learn mentality. Before rolling out new policies or tools to the entire organization, companies can experiment with pilot programs or small-scale implementations. For example, if employees suggest more flexible hours but the company is concerned about maintaining productivity, they could start by offering flexible work hours to one department or team and tracking the results.

Pilot programs allow organizations to test new strategies, monitor their effectiveness, and adjust accordingly before a full-scale implementation. This iterative approach reduces the risk of widespread disruptions while giving companies the opportunity to adapt and refine strategies over time.

3. Implementing Adjustments in Real-Time

In a remote or hybrid environment, real-time adjustments can be made more swiftly thanks to technology and digital communication tools. For example, if a manager receives feedback that team members feel disconnected, they can immediately adjust meeting frequencies, introduce new collaboration tools, or add team-building activities without needing to wait for quarterly reviews or annual surveys. The ability to pivot quickly based on real-time feedback is one of the biggest advantages of remote and hybrid work.

Similarly, if feedback reveals that a tool or system is causing inefficiencies, it can be replaced or optimized with minimal disruption. Tools like Asana, Trello, or Slack, which are central to remote work, can also be adjusted to reflect new workflows or processes in response to employee input.

4. Documenting and Sharing Learnings

An important part of iteration is capturing the lessons learned from each round of feedback and improvement. This documentation can be shared across teams and departments to ensure that all members are on the same page and that good practices are consistently adopted. It can also help create a knowledge base for future leaders, who can build on the lessons learned by others in the organization.

For example, if an organization successfully improves communication across time zones, documenting the strategies used and the results achieved can help other teams implement similar changes. Sharing these successes across the company helps create a culture of continuous improvement and encourages a proactive approach to change.

Staying Agile in the Face of Changing Work Dynamics

The landscape of remote and hybrid work is constantly evolving. As technology advances, societal expectations shift, and business needs change, organizations must remain agile and ready to adapt. An organization's ability to stay agile is what will ultimately determine its success in managing remote and hybrid teams in the long term.

1. Flexibility in Work Models

One of the key elements of staying agile in the face of changing dynamics is the ability to adjust work models quickly. For instance, if the needs of the business or employees change, companies should be able to modify their remote work policies without too much disruption. This could include adjusting hybrid work schedules, offering different levels of remote work flexibility, or changing the tools and technologies that support the work model.

For example, if an organization's initial hybrid model with fixed in-office days is no longer effective, they can experiment with more fluid, employee-driven scheduling options. This could be in response to employees wanting more autonomy or in reaction to changing business requirements that demand more flexibility.

2. Adapting to Technological Advancements

Technology is one of the most significant drivers of change in remote and hybrid work models. As new communication tools, collaboration platforms, and AI-powered solutions emerge, organizations must stay current with the latest technological innovations. The ability to implement new tools swiftly and effectively will help organizations maintain efficiency and productivity as they scale.

For example, adopting AI-based project management tools can help distribute workloads, monitor progress, and provide real-time insights into team performance. Virtual reality (VR) or augmented reality (AR) technologies can be integrated into collaboration strategies, offering more immersive meeting experiences that feel closer to in-person interactions.

3. Responding to Employee Expectations

Employees' expectations around remote work are changing rapidly. As more people experience the benefits of flexible work arrangements, they are becoming less willing to accept rigid in-office requirements. Staying agile means being open to feedback, monitoring employee sentiment, and adjusting work models as necessary to retain top talent and foster employee satisfaction.

For example, as the concept of a 4-day work week gains traction, companies may need to adjust their work models to meet employee demands for more time off. In response, remote and hybrid models might evolve to support this new trend, allowing employees to maintain work-life balance while still delivering results.

Continuous improvement is not just a goal—it is a necessity for maintaining effective and sustainable remote and hybrid work models. Feedback mechanisms, coupled with iteration and agile adaptation, ensure that organizations remain in tune with their employees' needs and that they can evolve as the business environment changes. By embracing continuous improvement as a core principle, companies can cultivate a dynamic, responsive workplace that is optimized for productivity, employee satisfaction, and long-term success.

18. Preparing for the Future

Future Skills for Remote Workers and Leaders

As the world continues to embrace remote and hybrid work models, the demand for new skills and competencies will rise. Both workers and leaders will need to develop specific abilities to navigate this evolving landscape successfully. These future skills are essential not only to enhance productivity but also to build a more adaptive, resilient workforce that can thrive in dynamic, distributed environments.

Future Skills for Remote Workers

1. Self-Discipline and Time Management Remote work requires individuals to be highly self-motivated, as they no longer have the physical structure and supervision of an office environment. Successful remote workers must be able to manage their time effectively, prioritize tasks, and maintain focus without direct oversight. The ability to set clear boundaries between work and personal life is critical in this regard, helping workers avoid burnout and maintain productivity.

Time management tools and techniques—such as Pomodoro, time-blocking, or digital task managers like Asana or Trello—will become increasingly valuable. Workers will need to develop a strong sense of autonomy to make these tools work to their full potential. Additionally, having the discipline to set aside dedicated periods for deep work versus collaborative tasks will be essential.

2. Digital Literacy and Tech Savviness With the proliferation of remote work technologies, workers must stay ahead of the

curve by honing their digital literacy skills. As the remote work landscape continues to be shaped by new software and platforms, individuals will need to be comfortable learning and adapting to a variety of tools used for communication, collaboration, project management, and cybersecurity.

Technologies such as artificial intelligence (AI), automation tools, cloud computing, and machine learning will require workers to not only understand how to use them but also leverage them to optimize their workflows. Familiarity with cybersecurity best practices—such as recognizing phishing attacks and using VPNs—will become second nature to remote workers as data protection remains a high priority.

3. Communication and Collaboration Effective communication will be one of the most important skills for remote workers in the future. While face-to-face interaction is limited, digital communication needs to be as clear, concise, and effective as possible. Remote workers will need to master various communication tools such as email, video conferencing (e.g., Zoom, Teams), instant messaging platforms (e.g., Slack), and collaborative spaces (e.g., Google Workspace, Microsoft 365).

However, communication skills are not just about knowing the tools; they also involve adjusting communication styles. Written communication must be more precise to reduce misunderstandings in an asynchronous environment. Remote workers will need to develop the ability to adjust their tone, use video effectively to convey emotions, and ensure clarity when providing feedback, especially when working across time zones.

4. Adaptability and Problem-Solving The remote work model is continuously evolving, with new tools, processes, and methods emerging regularly. Workers will need to be adaptable and resilient in the face of change. This will require developing a mindset that embraces experimentation, rapid learning, and flexibility.

Problem-solving skills will be vital as well. Remote work can present unique challenges—whether technical issues with remote tools, delays in communication across time zones, or personal struggles with isolation and motivation. Employees will need to cultivate a proactive, solution-oriented approach to resolving such issues quickly and effectively, without relying on others to manage them.

5. Emotional Intelligence (EI) Emotional intelligence (EI) will be crucial for remote workers to manage interpersonal relationships, both with peers and supervisors, in a virtual setting. EI involves understanding and managing one's own emotions as well as empathizing with others' emotions.

In a remote setting, it's harder to pick up on non-verbal cues and tone. Workers will need to develop strong emotional intelligence to navigate sensitive situations, foster positive relationships, and maintain team morale. High EI helps remote workers develop effective conflict resolution strategies, enhance their collaboration efforts, and promote a healthy and supportive work culture.

Future Skills for Remote Leaders

1. Virtual Leadership and Management Remote leaders must shift their traditional management styles to accommodate the nuances of virtual teams. They need to develop specific leadership skills for managing teams that may not have face-to-face interactions and who might work in different time zones, cultures, or locations. Successful remote leaders will need to be skilled at setting clear expectations, motivating their teams without physical presence, and communicating effectively through digital channels.

Leadership training will need to evolve to incorporate these new competencies, emphasizing emotional intelligence, trust-building, and virtual communication strategies. Being present in digital spaces—without micromanaging—is an essential skill. Leaders must be able to empower their team members while also maintaining accountability.

2. Cultural Competence and Inclusivity As remote work is often global, understanding and respecting diverse cultures and backgrounds will be a key skill for leaders. Leaders must be capable of fostering an inclusive environment where all voices are heard, regardless of geographic location, time zone, or cultural background. This includes understanding regional differences in communication styles, work habits, and expectations.

Leaders must also ensure that inclusivity goes beyond representation—it should encompass creating equitable opportunities for remote employees to succeed, offering the same resources, training, and growth opportunities regardless of location. Emphasizing diversity will also help create stronger, more creative teams that can solve problems from different perspectives.

3. Strategic Decision-Making in a Distributed Environment
Remote leaders will need to refine their decision-making abilities to lead dispersed teams effectively. This means adopting strategic thinking that can support the long-term success of remote operations, from scaling the workforce to evaluating new technology tools.

They will also need to make data-driven decisions by leveraging advanced analytics and performance metrics to assess team productivity, employee engagement, and organizational health. Leaders will need to integrate these insights into actionable strategies that support business goals while maintaining a healthy, collaborative, and resilient work environment.

4. Building and Sustaining a Remote Culture
Remote leaders must be adept at cultivating a positive company culture from afar. Organizational culture tends to thrive in physical spaces where employees can interact informally, but for remote teams, it requires intentional effort. A remote leader must find ways to keep employees motivated, connected, and aligned with the company's vision, even when they are miles apart.

Building a remote culture involves prioritizing communication, transparency, and recognition. Leaders will need to facilitate opportunities for social interaction, such as virtual coffee breaks, team-building activities, and online forums where employees can discuss topics outside of work. Additionally, they will need to reinforce values like trust, collaboration, and innovation, making sure employees feel engaged and valued.

5. Cybersecurity Leadership As remote work involves employees accessing company systems from various devices and locations, it presents unique cybersecurity challenges. Leaders must not only encourage safe practices among their teams but also stay up to date with cybersecurity threats and best practices to protect sensitive company data. This includes establishing and enforcing clear security policies, offering training on secure practices, and implementing tools that help detect and mitigate potential threats.

Leaders will need to balance the importance of security with the flexibility remote work provides, ensuring that employees have the tools and resources they need to work efficiently without compromising safety. Creating a culture of cybersecurity awareness will be a fundamental leadership skill in the future.

Building a Resilient Organization for Distributed Work

Building a resilient organization capable of succeeding in a distributed work environment involves preparing for the future, cultivating flexibility, and ensuring sustainability in operations. Resilient organizations are those that can quickly adapt to change, overcome challenges, and thrive despite obstacles. In the context of remote and hybrid work, resilience takes on several dimensions.

1. Embracing Flexibility in Work Models As remote and hybrid work models continue to evolve, organizations must create flexible policies and systems that can easily adapt to shifts in technology, employee needs, and market conditions. For example, a resilient organization will not only adopt remote work in response to a global crisis but will also be able to scale it up or down as required, whether by adjusting team structures, work hours, or geographic coverage.

Flexibility should also extend to the tools and technologies used to support remote work. Companies need to be prepared to quickly implement new tools or replace outdated systems that no longer serve their needs. By maintaining a flexible approach, organizations will be better equipped to respond to changing dynamics in the remote work landscape.

2. Building a Robust Digital Infrastructure A resilient remote organization relies heavily on a strong and secure digital infrastructure. This includes not only the right collaboration tools and software but also a reliable IT support system. Organizations should invest in technologies that ensure seamless communication, efficient task management, and secure data exchange.

Cloud computing, for instance, enables remote teams to collaborate in real time, share files securely, and access business-critical systems from anywhere. Building a robust digital infrastructure also involves regular training and support to ensure employees can leverage the technology effectively.

3. Continuously Evolving Leadership Practices Resilient organizations are built on effective leadership that is capable of adapting to changing circumstances. As remote and hybrid work models evolve, so too must the leadership approaches that guide teams. By continuously refining leadership practices, organizations can ensure that leaders are prepared to guide their teams through both expected and unforeseen challenges.

This includes providing leaders with ongoing training in remote team management, digital communication, conflict resolution, and organizational development. Additionally, leaders should be empowered to make decisions and drive change, allowing them to adapt quickly when new issues arise in the remote or hybrid work environment.

4. Encouraging Employee Well-being and Engagement Lastly, a resilient organization must prioritize employee well-being and engagement. As remote work can sometimes lead to feelings of isolation, burnout, or disconnection, organizations must implement systems and resources to support their employees' mental and physical health.

By offering flexible work arrangements, promoting regular breaks, and ensuring employees have access to resources like counseling or wellness programs, organizations can foster a resilient workforce. This, in turn, leads to higher productivity, job satisfaction, and long-term employee retention.

Preparing for the future of remote and hybrid work involves developing the necessary skills and systems that will allow both workers and leaders to thrive in these new environments. Remote workers need to master self-discipline, communication, and adaptability, while leaders must embrace virtual leadership, inclusivity, and strategic decision-making. Organizations, in turn, need to build flexible, resilient infrastructures that prioritize employee engagement, cybersecurity, and continuous growth. With the right preparation, both individuals and organizations can succeed in this evolving landscape and remain competitive in the global workforce of tomorrow.

19. Conclusion: Embracing Change in the Workplace

As we look to the future of work, it is evident that remote and hybrid work models are not just temporary responses to external events but are increasingly becoming the norm for many organizations across industries. The evolution of work has been accelerated by technological advancements, globalization, and the COVID-19 pandemic, which forced businesses to adapt rapidly to new ways of operating. This shift has fundamentally altered how we approach work, collaboration, and employee engagement, creating opportunities and challenges that require thoughtful strategies and resilient leadership.

Recap of Key Insights

Over the course of this book, we've explored the multifaceted nature of remote and hybrid work, highlighting the significant changes that these models bring to the workplace. The most important takeaway is that distributed work is not a one-size-fits-all approach. It is a dynamic and flexible framework that can be tailored to suit the needs of different organizations, industries, and teams.

1. Evolution of Work Models Remote and hybrid work are not just a response to an unprecedented global crisis, but part of a larger, ongoing shift in the world of work. The historical context shows that work models have always evolved—what we are experiencing today is simply a rapid acceleration of trends that were already in motion. The pandemic was a catalyst, but technology and globalization were already setting the stage for more distributed workforces. As businesses continue to embrace these models, the underlying drivers of change—such as technological advancements, employee demand for

flexibility, and cost-effective operations—remain powerful forces shaping the future of work.

2. Adapting Leadership for Remote and Hybrid Teams One of the core challenges in adopting remote work is the need for new leadership strategies. Traditional management styles, rooted in proximity and supervision, are not well-suited to virtual environments. Remote leadership requires a shift toward trust-based management, with a focus on empowering employees to work autonomously while maintaining clear communication and accountability. Leaders must also be adaptable, culturally competent, and capable of fostering collaboration without physical presence. The future of work will require leaders to continuously refine these skills and adapt to the ever-evolving nature of distributed work.

3. Building and Managing Distributed Teams A crucial part of remote work is the ability to build effective, engaged, and high-performing teams. Remote teams require unique approaches to recruitment, team dynamics, communication, and performance management. In this environment, team members need to be self-disciplined, digitally literate, and emotionally intelligent. Effective communication and the use of technology to create seamless workflows are essential to success. Leaders must also create a culture of inclusivity and diversity, ensuring that remote workers are not only productive but also feel supported and connected to the organization's values and mission.

4. Technology and Collaboration Tools The success of remote and hybrid work hinges on the effective use of technology.

Choosing the right collaboration platforms and communication tools is fundamental to keeping teams connected and productive. Whether it's for virtual meetings, project management, or sharing documents, technology allows remote teams to work as efficiently as if they were in the same physical space. However, technology also presents challenges, particularly regarding cybersecurity and data privacy. It is essential for businesses to invest in secure digital infrastructures and foster a culture of cybersecurity awareness among remote employees.

5. Work-Life Balance and Employee Well-being Remote work presents unique challenges to maintaining a healthy work-life balance. Without the physical separation between home and office, many employees struggle with overwork, isolation, and burnout. To thrive in this environment, companies must take proactive measures to support employee well-being. This includes offering mental health resources, encouraging regular breaks, and setting clear boundaries to prevent work from bleeding into personal time. Leaders must also foster a culture of flexibility, recognizing that each employee's circumstances are unique, and offering the support needed to help them succeed both professionally and personally.

6. Customizing Work Models for Different Organizations There is no universal approach to remote and hybrid work. The models need to be customized based on the unique needs of the organization, its culture, size, and industry. What works for a tech startup may not be effective for a multinational corporation, and what works for a small team might not scale to a large workforce. Leaders must take the time to assess their teams' needs, experiment with different models, and

continually adjust based on feedback. Creating tailored, adaptable policies will be critical to ensuring the success of remote and hybrid work long-term.

Call to Action for Leaders and Employees

As we embrace these new work models, both leaders and employees must be proactive and engaged in shaping the future of work. Leaders must foster an environment of trust, open communication, and continuous learning. They must invest in training, provide necessary resources, and ensure their teams are equipped to succeed in a distributed environment. For remote work to be truly effective, leaders must also be willing to evolve their leadership styles, embracing flexibility and innovation as they navigate the complexities of managing virtual teams.

Employees, too, must take responsibility for their own success in remote work environments. This means developing the skills necessary to work autonomously, manage their time effectively, and communicate clearly. Workers must embrace flexibility and adaptability, recognizing that remote work offers both freedom and responsibility. In return, organizations must offer the support, resources, and guidance employees need to thrive in these settings. Creating a sustainable and positive remote work culture is a shared responsibility.

In order to prepare for the future, both leaders and employees must remain agile and open to experimentation. Remote work models will continue to evolve, and staying ahead of these changes will require a commitment to continuous learning and adaptation. The workplace of tomorrow will be shaped by our willingness to innovate and embrace new ways of working. As organizations look to the future, they must not only focus on technological advancements but also on nurturing a resilient, engaged workforce capable of thriving in a distributed world.

Finally, embracing change in the workplace isn't just about adjusting to remote work. It's about rethinking how we work, collaborate, and lead in ways that are more inclusive, flexible, and sustainable. As organizations continue to redefine the workplace, the future of work lies in our collective ability to adapt, collaborate, and innovate.

By embracing these changes, we are not just adapting to a new way of working; we are creating a more inclusive, flexible, and resilient work environment for the future. The road ahead is full of opportunities for both employers and employees to redefine success, enhance productivity, and promote well-being in a way that wasn't possible in the traditional office environment. Let us embrace the future with a shared vision of growth, adaptability, and innovation, ready to meet the challenges of the evolving workplace head-on.

"The future of work is not defined by where you are, but by how you connect, collaborate, and innovate. Embrace the change, and you'll unlock limitless potential in yourself and your team."

www.ingramcontent.com/pod-product-compliance
Lightning Source LLC
Chambersburg PA
CBHW071026240526
45469CB00006BD/2112